Always Bear Left

**AND · OTHER · WAYS
TO · GET · THINGS · DONE
FASTER · AND · EASIER**

Also by Ken Cooper

NONVERBAL COMMUNICATION FOR BUSINESS SUCCESS
THE WORLD'S GREATEST BLACKJACK BOOK (with Lance Humble)
BODYBUSINESS

Always Bear Left

AND · OTHER · WAYS
TO · GET · THINGS · DONE
FASTER · AND · EASIER

Ken Cooper

A DELTA BOOK

A DELTA BOOK

Published by
Dell Publishing Co., Inc.
1 Dag Hammarskjold Plaza
New York, New York 10017

Delta ® TM 755118, Dell Publishing Co., Inc.

Printed in the United States of America

Designed by Judith Neuman

First printing—February 1982

Library of Congress Cataloging in Publication Data
Cooper, Ken.
Always bear left, and other ways to get things done faster and easier.
"A Delta book."
Bibliography: p.
Includes index.
1. Time management—United States. I. Title.
HN90.T5C66   646.7   81-15279
ISBN 0-440-50051-6   AACR2

to Mom,

No. 1 in the Insiders' Hall of Fame

Contents

Preface

Not too long ago I saw a cartoon which perfectly expressed how the world is today. A nervous gunman was pointing a pistol at the pilot of an airliner demanding, "Take this plane where it's supposed to go and get it there on time."

It seems like that's what it takes to get things done anymore. It's a crowded world filled with too many people trying to do the same thing at the same time. The "system" is eating us alive. The result is that things work slowly (when they work at all). Yet there seem to be a number of people who slide through life avoiding all the hassles and problems that plague the rest of us.

They are insiders who know how to get things done. They deal with the system and its people through their superior knowledge of how things operate. They are the "I can get it for you wholesale" of the life-style crowd. What they have done is to help us put together a book which shows you how to "live wholesale" too.

This book is actually a labor of love by hundreds of people. Early in the research cycle, I had my assistant busily ferreting out tips from a variety of sources. Suddenly the thought hit me, "Who wants to read a book on getting around the system that the author

had to write himself?" Following my own principles, the easiest, fastest, and cheapest way to write a
book was to let other people do the research for me.
Instead of finding tips, I could let the tips find me.

So I called a local newspaper about the book and
interested them in an article. The UPI picked up on
the article and sent it on the national wire, listing my
address. I copied the articles and sent them in a
package to over 400 radio stations suggesting they do
a phone interview and let people call in ideas or pet
peeves for which there was no answer. (See Appendix B.) I also gave out my address for those
wanting to send in ideas. As an incentive, I offered
to list in a special contributors' section anyone whose
idea was used. (See Appendix A.) Before long, my
mailbox was loaded with an incredible range of
ideas.

My researcher and I then spent our time verifying
the validity of the suggestions and tracking down
answers to the more popular pet peeves. Ideas that
were illegal (I have a great one for getting out of
parking tickets), unethical (such as getting out of jury
duty), or invalid for any reason were weeded out.
You can be certain that the ideas here have the
widest possible applicability and have been checked
to the best of our abilities.

If you have a pet peeve, then leaf through this
book. You're bound to find several ideas for solving
your problem. In fact, the top five pet peeves (as
listed here, according to my radio audiences) all have
straightforward solutions:
1. Waiting at the doctor's office
2. Waiting in bank lines
3. Getting a car repaired when promised

4. Phone solicitors
5. Incorrect computer bills

If you have a pet peeve or idea not included here, then see the last page of the book to find out what you can do about it.

I specifically wish to thank my researchers: Bobbie Knoedelseder, Karen Gentles, and Jane Dreeben. Their creativity and perseverance helped uncover many ideas. Thanks also to Mary Frances Cooper, Todd Kamp, Joanne Carr, and Husaini Saifee for their tremendous efforts in getting out the manuscript against a tight deadline. Their efforts insured we could pack every last tip into the manuscript. And thanks finally to my wife, Sue, who has put up with someone who can't go anywhere or do anything without stepping back to study how things operate.

"Lost time is never found again."
-*John H. Aughey*

1

Becoming an Insider

I recently finished an interesting little quiz, "How to Calculate Your Life Expectancy," which appeared on pages 975 and 976 in *The People's Almanac #2*. Everyone loves this type of exercise. We all want to dip into our future and see what it has in store for us—even if all we find out is how long our future will last. I'm no different. Based on my heredity and lifestyle, my number came up 77 years. Now years don't mean that much to me. I know what a year is, but I can't really comprehend exactly what one feels like. I tend to think in terms of weeks—or better yet, days and hours. So I sat down with my trusty calculator and found out that I should experience a lifetime consisting of 28,124 days or 674,982 hours (or approximately 40 million minutes or 2.5 billion seconds). When I think of 2.5 billion seconds, I am satisfied that I should have a long and fulfilling life.

But I next began to wonder how many of those 2.5 billion seconds were forever out of my grasp. As I write this, I have only 1.4 billion seconds remaining (only 23 million minutes or 390,000 hours). I've used over a billion seconds already and what do I have to show for them? How much fun have I had? How many of those seconds were a bust? a waste? an overall pain in the posterior?

I want my remaining 1.4 billion seconds to be more enjoyable, more interesting. I want to accomplish something of lasting value. I don't want to spend my precious future the way I've spent my past —parked in the middle of a superhighway turning the air hazy during rush hour, reading a two-year-old copy of something like *Dental Hygiene Today* in a waiting room, watching the other line move faster, or sprinting out of the bathroom to answer a phone call telling me my brick home needs new siding. No more of this for me. I want to be one of those skilled individuals who slide through life without ever making a right-angle turn. I want to be a pro corner-cutter in a world filled with weekend warriors. I want to be an insider in handling the events of life.

■ THE PHILOSOPHY OF EASIER, FASTER, AND CHEAPER

If someone asked me to describe the world, I would say, "Left." It's the only possible answer after listening to all the things in this life that are "Not right." To many, the "system," whatever that is, is a bit of security in a *Future Shock* world. This is not my attitude. The "system" is fine when it works. But when it doesn't, sometimes the only way to get things moving is to make it painful for others to keep messing with you. If you can negatively motivate them to get rid of you by taking care of your problem, then you have succeeded in a proper manner.

One of my favorite hints was sent to me by a woman with small children. Because of her husband's work schedule, she was always stuck with taking the car to the dealer for service. Because she had no return ride, she had to wait. It seemed like others got their cars on the rack first, particularly men. When she complained, she was told that the men worked and had to get back or that they had a previous appointment. After putting up with corraling the kids in the service waiting area, she came up with a perfect idea. The next time in for service, she brought along her children and a suitcase and sat down in the most comfortable spot in the main showroom. Then she took out her sewing. After a few more minutes she issued jelly sandwiches to the little darlings (bananas work just as well) and watched her offspring enjoy them all over the showroom. Amazingly, the car was ready soon after. She now carries her trusty suitcase nearly everywhere she goes if there might be a wait.

The Russians (reputed to be the only people in the world who can build old buildings) have a joke about the man going into one of the stores to buy a gift and finding two lines at the counter. One is overwhelmingly long, the other only discouragingly long. He gets in the merely discouragingly long line and asks the man ahead of him "What is this line for?"

"This is the line to get a special card which entitles one to first-class fast service," the man replies.

"And what is that larger line over there for?"

"Ah, that is the line of people who have the card."

Desperate times call for desperate jelly sandwiches. I get somewhat rabid about people wasting my time. I'm very jealous about each and every one of my 1.4 billion remaining seconds. I never know when today might be the day I climb on the metro bus and sit in front of Godzilla or when some car bumper might choose to get to know me more intimately. I don't want to spend my remaining days in line looking at someone's back.

All these books and articles that suggest ways to stay busy while waiting make me mad. It's like giving someone A•1 sauce after burning his steak. The clever insider learns not to wait at all.

I also want my life to be easier. The less energy I use to work, the more energy I will have to play. (This doesn't count mental energy. No one ever died from thinking too hard.) I want to be exhausted because I played the third set, not because I went the second mile. The workaholic is obscene, the playaholic sublime.

Finally, there is the little matter of money. For several years a large part of my salary was "respect," as in, "I always respected you, Ken." Then one day I foolishly took all those respects I had earned to the grocery store and used them to pay for a cart of groceries. You can imagine my dismay and surprise when they wouldn't let me have the food. Those respects didn't buy anything! There are lots of other mediums of exchange in use today—love, sex, status, but none which are more valid than the still popular method of keeping score, money.

My money requirements need not be excessive. Money translates into less work and more play, less drudgery and more fun, less waiting and more doing. Money is another form of time.

What I can't adjust to is the time expenditures which show no return. Waiting in line at the auto license bureau buys me nothing. Making three trips to the stores for something that still isn't in stock not only gives me no benefit, but it raises the price of the object dramatically. I'm throwing away my 1.4 billion seconds like a tipsy gambler in Las Vegas.

The philosophy here is to get the most out of your life by letting society get the least amount of your effort, time, and money. While rental car competitors show us how to merely check out faster, O. J. Simpson is flying through airports. If you can't manage the "system," it will certainly manage you. The difference is one of checking out or flying. The choice is yours.

■ IMPORTANT PEOPLE PSYCHOLOGY

Important People have it all over us mundane folks who carry fives and tens in our wallets. The reason is that IP's *know* they deserve good treatment, while we just *think* we do. Watch the way IP's saunter through a prestigious department store or waltz into a posh restaurant. Their whole manner says, "Okay, you tadpole, make certain you keep me happy."

To get in this class, say to yourself: MY LIFE IS IMPORTANT. ONCE MY BILLION SECONDS ARE GONE I CAN NEVER REGAIN THEM. I AM THROUGH LETTING PEOPLE STEAL PARTS OF MY LIFE.

Time is a resource. It can't be protected by converting it to traveler's checks (TIME—Don't leave home without it). It can't be saved like money or stockpiled like nuclear weapons. No one has the right to throw your seconds away for you.

I'm always amazed by people who rationalize waiting hours at the doctor's office by saying, "Well, he's so important and busy, I'm just happy he can see me today." WRONG! Medicine is a profession like any other. It requires more education than a teacher and less than an actuary. Medical care is a service. A doctor has no more right than a grocery store or a hamburger joint to make you wait several hours for service. What the medical profession currently has is an imbalance of supply and demand. As long as there are more sick people than doctors to take care of them, there will be waiting.

So if a doctor has no right to waste your time, then no one does. I'm not saying we have to be insufferable with everyone around us. It is merely better to *expect* only the best treatment from others. I refuse to beg someone to let me help them make a profit. And whenever I act this way I have no problem with service. I refuse to do business with anyone who has stolen some of my precious seconds through their indifference or neglect.

The other advantage Important People have over us is that they are unembarrassable. (Either that or their threshold of embarrassment is immeasurably high.) The average person will do just about anything to avoid a scene.

A typical ploy clerks use when we come to them with a problem they don't want to deal with is one which takes advantage of our reluctance to create a scene. They tell us, "Look, I know you have a problem there, but I've got too many people in line right now and you're holding things up. Could you move over there a minute and I'll take it to the manager when I get a moment." As you shift uneasily from foot to foot, people keep coming up to the counter to purchase items or to get help. Your "moment" turns into ten or fifteen minutes until you remind the clerk or have another clerk ask if you need help.

The Important Person never falls into this trap. The IP doesn't bother to turn around; he or she responds, "Well, they'll just have to wait since I was here first. I'm not moving a muscle until you get the manager over here and take care of this." The clerk now must decide if he should ignore you and wait on the others or take care of you. Since the clerk doesn't want a scene either, you are home free.

My pet peeve is having people cut in front of me in line. I don't mind telling the clerk in a loud voice that the person butted ahead and suggest that the clerk tell the person to wait his or her turn. My time is too important to let some rude twerp shift me back one position in line. When given the choice between an ugly scene or losing some of my precious seconds, let's hear it for conflict. MY LIFE IS IMPORTANT. ONCE MY BILLION SECONDS ARE GONE I CAN NEVER REGAIN THEM. I AM THROUGH LETTING PEOPLE STEAL PARTS OF MY LIFE.

■ YOUR CHOICES

If you are thinking, "Hey, it's about time I started respecting myself and my time," then you are well on the way to becoming an Important Person. These are the questions you should ask when considering nonplay activity.

● *Can I Ignore It?*

There are a whole host of duties in this world that will disappear if you leave them well enough alone. The worst thing you can do is accomplish them and then find out your efforts were unnecessary. Have you ever had someone call you up for information even though you're not the "right" person to answer the question? You track down the answer and then call back only to hear, "Thanks anyway, I got the answer somewhere else." It's no wonder you leave your handprints on the receiver. You've just had someone steal some of your seconds.

This philosophy makes a lovely poem:
> What you do not
> Do today,
> Given time
> May go away.

● *Can Someone Else Do It?*

According to the ancients, the gods have given us many gifts: love, humor, beauty, and so on. But the most important gift never had its own god. So we'll invent one, Drucker, who gives us the gift of delegation. I'm always amazed at the number of managers who work themselves to the bone while their underlings go home at 5:00 P.M. Something is amiss here. In the same category are parents who make their children's beds and pick up their clothes. I see a father with school-aged sons carrying out the trash and I think to myself that the kids will have him trained perfectly in a few more years.

What you must develop is a higher threshold of impatience. In *The Odd Couple*, Oscar never had to pick up anything because he lived with a bona fide compulsive who would do it for him. We don't have to treat everyone around us like slaves; we need only let them do the tasks they seem to derive pleasure from. Think of it as providing an opportunity for satisfaction. If your wife can't stand to see dirty dishes, by all means let her feel the sense of accomplishment of a clean countertop. If your husband wants the bills paid a certain way, give him the chance to write each check with a steady hand. This is true love.

If you have money that can be converted into time, then hire someone else to do your work. Around the home bring a housekeeper in once a week. Twice a year or so hire a heavy-duty cleaner to take care of windows, carpets, floors, the oven, etc. Use a laundry or diaper service, or hire teenagers for one-time jobs. Outside, use a lawn service or let one of the neighborhood children earn money by cutting and trimming. Let the kids paint your house or wax your car. Think of it as providing a social service while freeing you from unimaginable drudgery.

Commercially, have the local grocery roast your turkey and deliver it the day before a holiday. Order groceries over the phone and have them delivered. Get your gifts wrapped and mailed by the store. Shop by mail and let the vendor deliver to your door. The list is nearly endless. For a relatively small cost you can buy back hours and hours of time.

If you can't delegate everything, try to trade off duties. Think like Henry Ford—specialize. I don't wash dishes, my wife doesn't do yards. My wife likes a neat kitchen, I enjoy the outdoor exercise. Two neighbors of mine have a useful arrangement. One has a snowblower and keeps both their driveways clear in our moderate winters. The other has an electric air pump and tank which he uses to keep his neighbor's family bicycle tires inflated.

● *What Is the Least I Can Do?*

If all else fails and you actually end up having to do something, then do as little as possible. I'm a great believer in accomplishing nonplay tasks with mediocrity. For example, I want the type of house and yard that people drive by and say, "What house?" The guy up the street makes love to his lawn. (We call him Better Homes and Gardens.) He's out there night and day turning his grass into a cover girl. He actually had to mimeograph a sheet of his lawn care methods because so many people stopped to ask questions. This guy is crazy.

Another neighbor is afflicted with a brown thumb. He is the Angel of Death in the plant world. He does nothing to his lawn and his lawn responds in like manner.

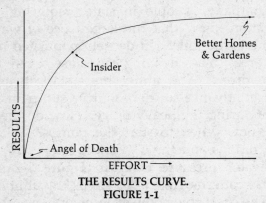

THE RESULTS CURVE.
FIGURE 1-1

My yard is in between those two extremes, existing in complete anonymity. It is neither so good nor so bad that anyone notices. More importantly, I'm in the best portion of the results curve. Figure 1-1 shows the basic relationship between effort and results. This is what time management experts call the "80–20 Rule." That is, 80 percent of the results come from only 20 percent of the effort. Too many of us are killing flies by dropping atom bombs.

I want to live my life at the top of the steep part of the results curve. I'm content with my 80 percent of the potential results because I need invest only 20 percent of the effort. My lawn has an acceptable amount of greenery, gets mowed once a week, gets fertilized three times a year, and is perfectly average. Consequently, I have to change the strings on my tennis racquet more frequently.

● Can I Live Off Peak?

Humans are creatures of habit. There are patterns to nearly everything we do. One of the most startling patterns comes, strangely enough, from the water company. People in states requiring water conservation know that the largest use of water in the home is the toilet. In densely populated metropolitan areas, mass flushing can cause severe water pressure drops. The utility must start its pumps enough in advance so there will be sufficient water pressure during the heavy usage. How do the companies know when to start the pumps? With the Nielsen ratings and the TV schedule.

The water pressure chart in Figure 1-2 shows heavy use patterns, called "TV drops" by utility engineers. The chart covers the evening of November 21, 1980. Trivia buffs will remember this as the evening the world finally found out that Kristin shot J. R. Ewing on "Dallas." That one hour show was seen by over 80 million viewers and piled up record Nielsen ratings. You can see the regular drops in pressure every fifteen minutes for the commercial breaks during the 9:00 P.M. to 10:00 P.M. (C.S.T.) showing. People were looking forward to the show because a lot of them made certain at 9:00 to relieve themselves

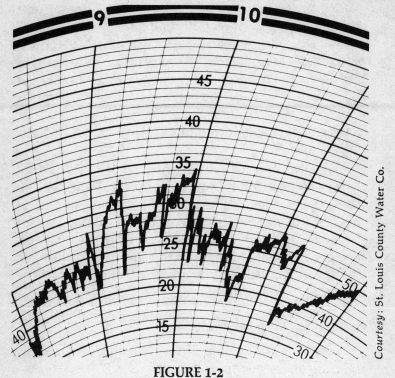

FIGURE 1-2

"Who Shot JR?" TV DROP.

before it started. Other significant TV drops occur at 10:30 at the end of the local news and at 11:15 when the Johnny Carson show begins to wind down and increases its commercial breaks.

A utility engineer mentioned in passing that the TV drops have been getting more consistent and larger during the week. They are even appearing on Friday nights for the first time ever. His interpretation is that more people are staying home because of the recession-poor economy.

TV has affected other businesses, too. Restaurants recognize that Monday nights during the football season will be slow because of "Monday Night Football." An emergency room physician told me that during football season Monday evenings are always slow. Fans would rather let their kids bleed on the floor than miss seeing if the game goes into overtime. "Things are really dead then," the doctor told me with a grin.

Learn to avoid the crowd. Instead of waiting until the last day of the month to get an auto license, an insider goes the 15th. Instead of waiting in line at the 7:00 P.M. movie, insiders meet after work and see the 5:00 rush hour show, then go out to eat. Insiders buy next year's Christmas cards in January and get their heaters checked in August. All it takes is a little planning.

● *Can I Batch Up My Work?*

There is a certain amount of lost time with every task. Business people call it "overhead" or "setup." By batching up your work you minimize the time wasted in overhead. For example, if you make three trips to run three errands you are probably driving over some of the same roads each trip. You can do all three errands in one trip faster than in three trips because you only travel those roads once.

If you are outside washing the car, wash the other car, too. You are already wet, the hose is out, and the bucket is still full of soapy water. It doesn't make sense to wash one car Tuesday and the other Wednesday. (Of course, it makes better sense to not wash it at all.) By batching the washing job, you change clothes, mix the soap, get the hose out, then dry off and change back only once instead of twice.

The trick is to think like Amoco Oil. We pump gas fifteen or twenty gallons a tank, but they cook it up about 3 million gallons at a time. There is efficiency in volume because it minimizes setup and overhead. Concentrate on generating volume by batching up your nonplay duties whenever possible.

If you ask these questions whenever you are faced with a request for some of your valuable seconds, then you are well on your way. The late Karl Wallenda said, "Life is on the wire, the rest is just waiting." What counts is what we enjoy doing. The tips that follow will all help you spend more time "on the wire."

"Have you noticed how long it takes to see a doctor these days? They have replaced those old magazines in the waiting rooms . . . with full-length novels."

—Lou Erickson

2

Concerning Your Body

This year saw three of the all-time great players inducted into the professional football Hall of Fame. I was saddened to see that Herb Adderly, Jim Otto, and Bob Lilly creaked up the stairs to receive their awards. All three had permanently damaged "wheels," leg injuries which visibly reduced their mobility. In an interview after the ceremony, Jim Otto spoke with regret about what football had done to his body.

There are few givens in life, but one of them is the chassis we must spend our life inside. While many people abuse their bodies by sniffing, puffing, shooting, gulping, popping, or inhaling, more and more we are realizing that if we want to get our full share of seconds we had better take care of the body we have. That's why there will always be a place in any society for a medicine man, shaman, or the modern-day version, the doctor.

■ DEALING WITH THE HEALTH CARE SYSTEM

A question frequently asked in my radio appearances soliciting ideas for the book was, "What is the most common pet peeve?" This is easy to answer since the first thing most people say after hearing about the book is, "Say, what a great idea. Listen, do you have any ideas about how not to wait at the doctor's office?"

Nothing burns us up more than having to wait for the opportunity to make some doctor rich! Not only that, a doctor with the social sensitivities of a brick explains what's wrong with us in language that would put Howard Cosell to shame. Then the doctor prescribes medicines with names like Albanian revolutionaries that have made their way onto the market by not killing rats and convicts. If I hadn't seen a CAT Scanner in operation, I'd swear we weren't too far away from medicinal bleeding and goat bones thrown in the dirt. Still, there are some hints in dealing with the medical industry.

■ AVOID WAITING AT THE DOCTOR'S OFFICE

None of these methods comes with a guarantee, but studious application of several of them should reduce the amount of time you spend in the waiting room. Who wants to sit in a room with all those sick people anyway?

● *Get the First Appointment in the Morning*

This is the best approach if the doctor doesn't have hospital rounds in the morning. Even if he is late from rounds, you won't have to wait longer than anyone else. Arrive early. Typically the nursing staff shows up before the doctor is scheduled to see patients. The doctor frequently gets there through a side door sometime during that interval and relaxes, slugging down his morning coffee and reading *The Wall Street Journal* to see how his tax shelters are faring. I tell the nurses that I'm in a desperate hurry and that I know the doctor is back there. I then ask if the doctor would do me a favor and take me immediately. I've often gotten out of the office before the second patient ever arrives.

● Get the Day's Last Appointment

When you don't have the time to set up an early appointment, try to squeeze in right before closing. Call about 4:30 or so and ask if they couldn't see just *one* more sickie. Offer to drive right over and promise to talk fast so the physician won't have to spend too much time.

● Call Ahead and Shift Your Appointment

If you are stuck with an appointment in the middle of the day, call about an hour before and ask whether the doctor is on schedule. If not, ask how much of a delay there is. If it is an hour, for example, shift your appointment an hour later and mention that you expect to then be taken on arrival. Explain that you, too, are a professional and that your time is extremely valuable. Say that you are willing to modify your schedule and come in later but you expect the doctor to reciprocate. The key point you want to get across to the nurse is not that you require any specific time, but that you *will not wait*. Most nurses find this reasonable and will do their best to accommodate you.

If you end up waiting anyway, mention what the nurses promised you to the doctor. Let him know you feel it is unprofessional and you thought he ought to know about it. Don't gripe, though, if you are behind an emergency. Someday YOU may break your ankle and be glad someone saw you right away.

● *Bill Doctor for Waiting Time*

Lots of "intimidation experts" suggest you bill the doctor for any waiting time at an appropriately high fee and deduct it from your bill payment. The idea is that the doctor will immediately respect you more and treat you immediately next visit. While this may work in some cases, every doctor has had several patients try this already. This suggestion is a terrific way to have to find a new physician. Lots of doctors don't even see the money or look at the finances. You may find yourself with the doctor's bill collection agency panting after you and screwing up your credit rating.

The time to try the billing routine is after doing the reschedule trick above when the nurse does not follow through. Tell her *then* that you intend to bill the next time she promises you will get in right away and then keeps you waiting. When you come in again, remind her of your previous promise brought about by the unfortunate wait last time, and say that you hope you won't have your busy schedule blown again. Once you get the nurse trained properly, you won't have further nonemergency waits.

● *Don't Downplay How You Feel*

One person suggested collapsing in the waiting room. True, that gets lots of action. But I don't think it's fair to fake an emergency when people with legitimate illnesses are waiting. By the same token, don't let Aunt Minnie with the terminal hangnail bust in ahead of you if you need help. I've seen people about to pass out desperately trying to wait their turn because of a misplaced sense of fair play. If you have what the childbirth professionals call "discomfort" (you and I call it PAIN), don't sit there and suffer.

● *Get Medical Assistance Over the Phone*

If you have some minor ailment that doesn't require you to see the doctor, don't be embarrassed to call for advice and medicine. Most doctors will speak to patients when they call or will call back at specific times. Other doctors refuse to give this type of "free" service. My feelings are that a doctor's most precious resource is time. He only has one body and only so many hours in the day. I'm more than willing to have the doctor charge me some part of an office visit for a phone call answer and phoning a prescription. I have used his or her time and have also saved an enormous amount of my own. In addition, I didn't have to go to the trouble of dragging my sick chassis over there to hack around in the waiting room. That's worth something. If the nurse balks at letting you talk to the doctor, remind her you don't mind being billed.

■ GETTING INSURANCE FORMS FILLED OUT

Insurance forms are the athlete's foot of a medical practice. The result is that forms are lost, returned late, or returned incomplete so that they have to be sent in again.

● *Include a Stamped Self-Addressed Envelope*

An envelope and stamp aren't much to you, but multiply them by up to 100 each day and you see what the typical doctor faces. You'll save the doctor time and money plus earn appreciation at a negligible cost to yourself. You will also minimize the chance of the form getting lost or mailed out improperly.

● *Mark Spots on Form to Be Completed*

"X" each line the doctor should complete with a red felt-tip pen. When in doubt, go ahead and mark it. This will reduce the chance of getting an incomplete form back.

■ BUSY AND SLACK PERIODS BY MEDICAL SPECIALTY

Much of our medical care is elective, i.e., we can choose when it will occur. Following is a list of the common medical specialties and their patient patterns so that you can find slack periods and avoid busy times.

Chiropractors

Early autumn is the busy season as football injuries pile up and weekend warriors overtax their once-proud bodies. Patient load lightens during the holidays or in bad weather. During the week early afternoons are busiest with evenings and Saturday morning usually light.

Dentists

Few people want to have someone scraping and drilling during the holidays. December is usually the slowest month. During the week, early morning and late afternoon are busy while lunchtime is least busy.

General Practitioners

A GP's patient load shows no seasonality. Lighter days (if there are any at all) are Tuesday and Thursday and busier days Monday and Friday. The Monday folk want to get off work and the Friday folk want to get healed on company time to avoid messing up the weekend.

Hearing Aid Services

Wintertime is always slow. The older clientele has a much harder time getting out and will postpone a visit to the office until better weather.

Obstetricians

Late spring and early summer are the busy times, midsummer the slowest. August and November seem to have more deliveries—I guess people are too busy during the Christmas holidays. You can never be sure with an OB, but Friday afternoons usually make for the best office visits.

Optometrists

Midwinter or early spring are slack periods. Optometrists are busiest in late spring when income tax refunds come back or in early fall when children need glasses for school.

Pediatricians

Pediatricians are busy all the time. The peak period, if you can differentiate between an atomic bomb and our sun going supernova, is fall, when school and athletic exams are required. The slowest day, if there is such a thing, is usually Thursday.

Pharmacists

Late summer months show the least demand for medicine, harsh Januaries show the greatest demand. (Winter is very hard on the elderly.) During the week, evenings are slow with midmorning and late afternoon busy.

Podiatrists

December is the slow month. Other than that one month, the podiatrist sees a fairly regular patient demand in what is typically not a rushed practice.

Psychologists

Their schedule is slowest in early fall and busiest before and after Christmas. The holiday season brings out depression and the postholiday business environment is typically the worst for unemployment.

Radiologists

Ask a doctor what the ideal specialty is and most will say radiology. The hours are manageable, the fees are in the ball park, and "reading film" isn't as messy or time consuming as some of the other specialties. The radiologist is basically dependent on other doctors who require X rays. Vacation time is slowest because fewer doctors are seeing fewer patients. During the week, 7:00 to 9:00 A.M. is usually open since few doctors have office hours this early and therefore don't refer patients then.

■ MEDICAL SUPPLIES

We've come a long way since bat ears, frog innards, and ground-up dandelions. The pharmaceutical industry is a giant, dispensing all types of public and prescription drugs. With a little background information you can dramatically reduce your medicine bills.

● *Ask the Doctor for Cheapest or Generic Drugs*

You can go into any drugstore and find a brand-name product like One-An-Eon Vitamins. This is a brand-name product with a brand-name price to pay off all that advertising for brand-name recognition. Sitting right next to it in the same shaped bottle with exactly the same contents listed on the label is normally something like Dead Roach Vitamins. It has a price tag only half as much as its famous competitor. Dead Roach Vitamins is an example of a generic name.

The same concept works for prescription drugs. Companies spend millions of dollars promoting drugs by name, and then also sell quantities under a generic name, or competitors may make an equivalent drug. Your doctor doesn't always take the time he should to save you money, so _ask_ whenever you get a prescription if he is listing the generic drug, or if none is available, if he is listing the cheapest version. Make certain you see "or g.e." (or generic equivalent) at the end of the prescription. Then check with the pharmacist to see if there are any money-saving alternatives.

● **Have the Doctor Phone in the Prescription**

Ask your doctor if he wouldn't mind phoning in your prescription. Make it easy on the doctor and have the phone number handy on your questions list. Again, if you've established the relationship as a fellow "professional," this should not be a problem. This way the order will be ready when you get there. If the doctor will phone in, then you have the option of avoiding the drugstore entirely. Most stores will deliver at no extra charge. You may have to wait a few hours but you will save a trip.

● **Quiz the Pharmacist About the Prescription**

Many times the busy physician fails to mention a key tidbit about the medicine to be used. Maybe the magic pill will make you bark like a dog if you mix it with coffee or whatever. Ask the pharmacist about any side effects, restrictions, or tips on usage to make certain the doctor didn't skip a key fact. Many medicines have special shelf lives, mix poorly with certain foods, or go down smoother at certain times of the day.

● *Getting Medicine Down Kids*

○ *Use an empty nipple for infants*

I can't tell you how many babies I've seen with medicine stains on their little shirts. Drugstores give out these tubelike medicine spoons that guarantee an active little tongue can expel more than half the dose. The easiest way to get medicine down the pipe is to get the little one started sucking an empty nipple and then pour the dose in the nipple. The baby swallows the goop before it knows what happened.

○ *Put the dose in perspective*

The nipple trick won't work with kids once their IQ hits the power curve. The best way to give medicine to the thinkers is to lay everything out in DOUBLE doses on the counter. If one tablespoon is required, fill up two spoons and set them on the table. If two pills are necessary, set out four. Then bring the child in.

Any kid worth his or her respective aggravation factor will begin to thrash at this time. After putting up a token fight, allow yourself to be bargained down to one spoon or two pills. Return the remainder to the bottle.

■ DEALING WITH AN EMERGENCY ROOM

Hospital ER's see just about every human ailment from psychosomatic aches to life-ending traumas. They have their good and bad points just like any other service. On the good side, lives are saved almost daily. On the bad side, women in labor have been turned away to give birth in the parking lot because their insurance was not adequate. (One private hospital in St. Louis even sent a man with a knife in his back to the city hospital. The explanation was that the move wasn't life threatening and the city doctors could just as easily remove the knife.)

● *Avoid Postdinnertime and Bedtime*

The ER typically experiences late afternoon and postdinnertime rushes. Body temperature tends to rise in the afternoon and tired workers are more liable to injure themselves. Dinnertime is a lull because the sick ones have to hang on while the healthy ones stoke up. After the eats are downed the ill are brought in.

Bedtime is always a busy period. It's not that parents are negligent, it's just that they don't mind a child being sick while they are up. But when the child won't go to sleep due to illness, the parents finally realize the child will have to see a doctor if the adults are going to get any sleep.

● *Avoid the ER After "Big Events"*

As you read in Chapter 1, the slowest time of the week is during "Monday Night Football." Along the same lines, the slowest time of the year is Super Bowl Sunday. During the game everyone is in front of the TV instead of hurting themselves. And the sick have to suffer until the viewers see the finale and determine who owes how much to whom. According to one ER physician, "After the Super Bowl, all hell breaks loose." The same pattern is observed with "Who Shot J.R.?" and other such events.

● *Be Careful on Weekends and Holidays*

Weekends generally show a reduced sickness load and a greatly increased accident rate. Part of this also carries over into the Monday load. The Sunday crowd comes in because they don't want to miss work, and the Monday crowd wants an excuse for not going. They all get their wish at three times the going rate.

● *Be Assertive*

People can sit in agony with broken bones while the ER doctors are busily cutting away torn toenails and other minor injuries. This is usually not the doctors' fault since the nurses do most of the screening. Blood isn't even a guarantee of quick treatment. I've seen nurses hand out a compress and let the person sit for an hour. If you are in doubt, go up to the desk and firmly state your case. One father whose son sat for an hour in tremendous pain with a broken bone ended up calling the hospital administrator and getting him down to the ER. The nurses later told the man it was the first time the administrator had even *seen* the ER in his three years there. The son got immediate treatment.

● *Get the Name of Everyone Who Handles You*

In the typical trip to the ER, the last thing you are is organized. Yet it is important to get everyone's name—whether nurse or doctor. This is the only way you will be able to handle any later problems. Also write down what the doctors are telling you and make them explain what is happening (if there is time).

I was once kept waiting an extra hour and a half while a special blood test was run. My son had hurt his knee falling down, so I couldn't understand why the test was necessary. Nonetheless, I wrote the test information down and wrote a letter of complaint when the bill arrived. When the smoke cleared, it turned out the doctor was doing a special research project on a rare blood disease and scheduled the test whenever there was the slightest chance of finding another subject for his study. It was too late to regain my time, but I didn't pay for the test and this was only because I had gotten all the details and times. Most of this should be on the medical record, but sometimes the record is not clear.

● *When in Doubt, Ask for a Second Opinion*

When it comes down to doing something permanent to the last body we're ever going to be issued, it becomes worthwhile to get a second opinion. Of course, if your heart has been on strike for several minutes, then cancel that last bit of advice. But don't be rushed into something that is unclear to you just because you are in the emergency room. If there is time, get in touch with your family doctor. He may do nothing more than explain what is happening, but it is still worth your trouble (and his). No reputable physician will ever mind your seeking a medical opinion. If medicine were an exact science, we'd all go to an R2-D2 sitting in a corner of Sears. (By the way, this advice goes for any other medical service. When in doubt, check it out with another doctor or two.)

● *Shop for an ER*

With three small children, I might as well run a
tab at the ER and let them bill me monthly. When we
take so much time to carefully choose our other
doctors, it doesn't make sense to not carefully select
the best ER. All ER facilities must meet certain stand-
ards, but some are better equipped than others.
Certain hospitals are also staffed with emergency
physicians, a recently established medical specialty.
When you go to visit someone in the hospital, take
time to visit the ER facilities. You won't get a guided
tour, but you will get a feel for the place.

Ask your family doctor which hospital ER's are
best. He may be able to give you important background information. For example, there are five hospitals within fifteen minutes of my home. One in
particular is noted throughout the metropolitan area
as having the best plastic surgeons, and for doing the
best job on facial injuries. This fact came in handy
when one of the neighborhood children decided to
introduce my son's head to a rock.

● *Follow Up with Your Own Doctor*

After an ER visit, it is a good idea to follow up with
an office visit to your regular doctor. This gives your
doctor an opportunity to check progress, review
medications, and guide further treatment. It also as-
sures that the incident will become part of your
permanent medical record on file. This is an additional expense, but I'll admit to a bias toward spending a few dollars on maintaining my chassis. My
local National Automotive Parts Association dealer
has told me there is no factory grade replacement.

■ HOSPITAL CARE

Going to the hospital is about as much fun as showing up for work and finding Mike Wallace in your waiting room or having Chuck Barris ask you to be on one of his shows. Yet there are a few tips that can help smooth your stay.

● *Schedule Elective Surgery Off Peak*

Occupancy rates vary depending upon the facility. A major acute-care hospital will have few peaks and valleys in patient load while averaging high 90 percent occupancy year around. If there are any valleys in occupancy, they are shortly before and after holidays. If there is a busy period, it is during summer vacations when people elect to fix up the plumbing when it will be more fun off work recuperating.

● *Be Nice While You're There*

Most people have no concept of what a nonjoy it is to deal with sick people day after day. (The only crowd that whines more are casino gamblers.) It's not the patients' fault—they are in a strange, frightening place under worrisome circumstances. Yet the work environment for nurses and administrative personnel is acidic.

A nurse taking one of my courses counted up the number of critical or complaining comments she heard in an average day and totaled 72. This works out to about one slam every five minutes.

"Nurse, why didn't you get here when I called?"

"Nurse, this bed is too high."

"Nurse, what do I have to do to get you to answer that buzzer, sit on it?"

"Nurse, why doesn't my son/grandmother/uncle/ spouse have another blanket?"

This is the normal dose. If you are a professional carper, plan to spend lots of time by yourself. While the nurses don't like to admit it, negative patients tend to be avoided. This is one situation where it doesn't pay to make it painful to do business with you. Give the help a break and try to remain cheerful. You'll be such an oddball the staff will love you.

● *To Get Nursing Help*

Still, even if you are Merry Sunshine incarnate, you may occasionally feel like the guy doing the car commercial atop the desert butte. If you can't break one of the nurses free from her pinochle game, or whatever else nurses do to entertain themselves at the station, then here are a few ideas:

○ *Lean on your button*

This depends upon the technology of your hospital. Some of the button systems make a noise at the nurses' station—others merely turn on a light. If it's the former, you're in luck. Newer hospitals have intercoms built into the call module, which is the best of all situations.

○ *Go get it yourself*

Nothing gets the nurses' attention faster than your wandering around, rummaging through hospital supplies looking for whatever you need. The price is a lesson in manners accompanied by some serious finger-wagging, but the results may be worth it.

○ *Scream for it*

Don't yell anything dangerous such as "Help" or "Fire"—yell for what you need. Not only does it create a satisfying ruckus which generates some action, but it is an excellent way to rid yourself of those common "I'm in the hospital" anxieties. Once again, the price is a bit of schoolmarming from the nurses.

○ *Call from your room phone*

The nurses may not mind your pounding away on your call button, but they don't want to miss an outside call from the Important Person in their life. It amazes me to see people complaining that they can't get hold of a nurse when they are sitting eighteen inches from a phone. Dial for an outside line, next dial the hospital (the number is always on the phone), and then ask for the ninth floor nurses' station (or wherever you are). When you get a breathing hominid on the other end of the line, state your needs and request they get rolling.

Sometimes getting proper medical care, whether at a doctor's office, a hospital ER, or as an in-patient, seems like watching a Three Stooges' rerun. Just try to keep in mind that these folks are only professionals and not deities. Your time is just as valuable to you as theirs is to them. All seconds are equal.

■ **PERSONAL SAFETY**

The mere fact that personal safety should be addressed here says quite a bit about the recent changes in our cities. Violence and crime have always been with us, but never so publicly and never in such great volume. Self-defense classes are increasingly popular. The stores are full of all sorts of self-defense gizmos from a simple whistle to an electronic alarm, and weapons from a pointed comb to chemical sprays. Yet there are other simple techniques which just might help you.

● *Look Confident*

The August 1980 issue of *Psychology Today* included a study done by two New York psychologists, Betty Grayson and Morris Stein. They secretly videotaped sixty New York City pedestrians for six to eight seconds each—approximately the time a potential mugger has to size up a victim. The tapes were shown first to a pilot group of twelve prisoners convicted of assault on strangers and later to another fifty-three convicted muggers. The criminals were asked to rate each pedestrian on a one to ten scale for "muggability." At least half the viewers rated the same twenty people as potentially easy victims and at least half rated nineteen others as the least likely victims.

The researchers then had a trained dance analyst study the "muggables" to see what movements the muggers were keying on. Generally, muggables' strides were off-sized—either too long or too short. They moved awkwardly, sometimes with their arms swinging out of sync with their leg movements. The steps they took were more flat-footed, instead of rocking forward from heel to toe with each stride.

In checking with police officers in my classes, I was told crime victims often exhibit lack of confidence. They are also not as aware of what is going on around them. A crook is typically nervous or afraid— or often on drugs. All he wants is an easy victim who will cause the least amount of trouble. Someone who is physically fit, alert, and walking confidently stands the least chance of attracting a mugger when there are other potentially less troublesome victims walking by every few minutes.

● *Cooperate Quietly with a Robber*

If a thief demands your money, give it to him quickly and quietly. Remember his mental state. If he's armed, the excitement alone will have the trigger half-pulled. Experts recommend you don't plead, argue, or chatter. Pass on the money and let him take off. No amount of money is more important than your life.

If you want something to do during a robbery other than age at an increased rate, concentrate on remembering the description of the robber. You needn't scan the person top to bottom while moving your lips. Just pick out the key body and facial features along with a general description of the person. This will be of tremendous help to the police. Your accurate description may mean the difference between catching or missing a crook. Ultimately you may save some stranger's life by getting another crook off the streets.

● *Carry a Dummy Wallet*

A building inspector who worked in rough neighborhoods passed on the idea of carrying a dummy wallet. A travel agent also used this trick when in a strange country. A thief rarely takes the time to search victims or have them empty every pocket or purse. You can keep an old wallet which has *some* money (never empty, for this will frustrate the robber) and several *out of date* credit cards, or better yet, old ID cards for realism. If you are accosted, toss this over and don't volunteer that you have another wallet.

● *Tell Him You Have the Flu, Diarrhea, or Are Going to Vomit*

The experts are divided about how to handle assaults—particularly a sexual assault. Some suggest passively going along with the assailant to minimize the risk of further injury. Others suggest fighting until the attack is too much trouble. An ingenious approach that several women have used and had work is to take the attacker totally off guard. Tell him you have the flu and were just going home to go to bed. One lady with real presence of mind told the man, "I can't stop you. But if you get my flu it will serve you right." After looking at her, he turned and ran off. If the mention of flu doesn't do the trick, try telling him you are having diarrhea and have to get home quickly.

Another woman told me she yelled out in panic as the man grabbed her (she said it wasn't too hard to pretend), "Oh, my God, I'm going to vomit." The key word here is "vomit." "Throw up" or "upchuck" don't seem to have the emotional impact of "vomit." Then the woman made retching sounds. She said the man acted like he was grabbing a leper and took off.

■ ADJUSTING TO YOUR BODY CYCLES

Mention "body cycles" to people and they immediately think of biorhythms, astrology charts, or other such nonsense. Yet scientists have been studying how time affects our physical rhythms. For example, in one experiment subjects were isolated from any time indicators such as the sun rising or seeing a clock. The result was that they adapted a twenty-six hour day. This seems to be "normal" for humans. There are other important cycles in our lives. Two of the most important are our sleep cycles and our personal productivity and alertness curves.

● *Schedule Your Day to Match Your Productivity and Alertness Curve*

In my seminars, I noticed there were fairly predictable patterns of attentiveness and efficiency in my audiences. I decided to survey each class for its own particular cycle to see if I could schedule the course activities to fit its particular composite pattern. Each

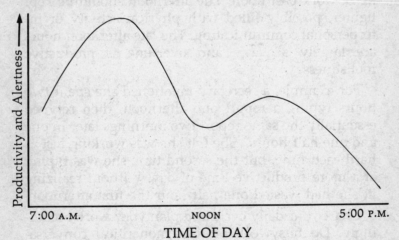

TIME OF DAY

COMPOSITE PRODUCTIVITY AND ALERTNESS CURVE.
FIGURE 2-1

person rated his or her productivity or alertness from 1 to 10 on an hourly basis from 7:00 A.M. to 6:00 P.M. Figure 2-1 shows the composite ratings for approximately 2,000 adults surveyed.

The chart illustrates several patterns. Morning start-up is slow. The 9:00 A.M. to 11:00 A.M. interval is the best time for attentiveness. People crash right before lunch as fatigue and low blood sugar take over and start up sluggishly afterward only to crash once again in late afternoon. Finally, the best of the afternoon is hardly better than the worst of the morning.

The scheduling requirements are obvious. People require light early warmup to get the neurons flowing. The midmorning is best for heavy thinking requiring high attention or reactive listening. Breaks should be more frequent as lunch approaches—and NEVER work past noon! The afternoon should be kept lighter, possibly filled with physical activity or interpersonal communicating. The late afternoon hours are largely a waste and overtime is productive foolishness.

For example, a secretary mentioned she spent two hours typing a report one afternoon, then retyped essentially the same report two mornings later in one and one half hours. She felt she was working just as hard each time, but the second time she was typing at a more productive time of day. Without realizing it, she had wasted one half hour the first afternoon.

Chart your daily cycle and plan your work accordingly. Do busywork or have noncritical conversations during low periods. Do your planning and thinking during alertness peaks. You may be wasting precious seconds strictly because of reduced productivity.

● *If You Are a Night Person*

There is one qualification to Figure 2-1. The chart is typical of a "day person"—someone who wakes up bright and alert. If a day person wants to get more done, he or she gets up earlier. This represents about two-thirds of the population. The other third, however, show about equal productivity for morning and afternoon, with both in the lower range. This other third consists of "night people"—those who get rolling after dinner and stay up later to get more done. Figure 2-2 illustrates this pattern. Unfortunately for night people, they exist in a day world.

If night people extend their ratings beyond the dinner hours, Figure 2-2 is the result. The night

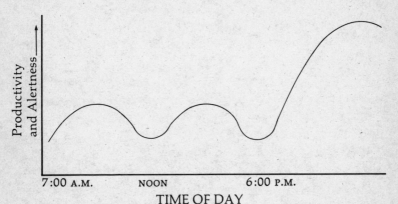

TIME OF DAY

"NIGHT PERSON" PRODUCTIVITY AND ALERTNESS CURVE.

FIGURE 2-2

person is not at a productive peak during any of the normal day-person work hours. The night person wakes up feeling like a 45 rpm record played at 33⅓. The air seems to have a consistency of molasses and the eyes seem to be watching a Rod Serling show. The same general advice on planning activities applies to night people—schedule to peaks—to the extent that this is possible for you.

P.S. The only way to change your alertness pattern is to have a baby. Then you are NEVER at a peak.

So these are a few hints on keeping your body functioning and safe, and on helping it do more for you. It's all you've got, and it will do just fine if you respect it and have everyone else treat it right.

"Home is where you can scratch any place that itches."

–Evan Esar

3

The Important Person at Home

The human animal has always felt something special about its home. As Bret Harte pointed out, "Nobody shoulders a rifle in defense of a boarding house." Not only does our home have a special place in our heart, it has an even more important place in our pocketbook. For most of us, our home is the most important investment we ever make. As such, we must care for it wisely.

■ HOME INSURANCE

Each day it seems the papers or news programs show another fire or natural disaster. Floods ravage entire valleys. Forest fires wipe out complete housing tracts in California. But with insurance coverage we need never worry about being financially, if not emotionally, wiped out by the loss of our home. Wrong again. Homeowners lose thousands of dollars because of poor planning and lack of information.

● *Keep Pace with Inflation*

At a 10 percent inflation rate, the home you bought seven years ago now costs twice as much to replace. You must insure the total value of your home and its contents at *current* prices, not what you paid for them. And with the inflation rate staying high, your home policy should be reviewed annually.

● *Insure Furnishings and Valuables for* Replacement *Costs*

Many older policies are written to reimburse you for the depreciated value of your possessions. Your $400 TV set may only be worth $200 now after several years of heavy sit-com use. But you may have to spend $600 to replace the TV, which means a net out-of-pocket loss of $400 *after insurance*. It's a better idea to insure your possessions for their *replacement* value, i.e., what you would have to spend today to replace all your possessions, regardless of their age, with equivalent but new models.

Items listed separately should be reviewed periodically. Jewelry has been going up in value so quickly that many owners have been getting the pieces appraised for insurance purposes every several months.

● *Photograph Your Valuables*

Stroll through your domicile and look at all the clothes, decorations, and general stuff littering the floor and shelves. If your home was nothing more than an oversized charcoal briquet after a fire, could you list each and every item lost in the blaze? You'd undoubtedly overlook items worth thousands of dollars. The fastest and easiest way to establish home contents for insurance purposes (if you didn't keep receipts) is to photograph *all* your possessions.

Photograph everything. Get each room from several angles so you include every piece of furniture and every wall decoration. Shoot the inside of every closet. For important details, shoot close up and include something to show size. For room pictures, a yardstick is suitable; for small detail shots a foot ruler will work. Pose small items against a backdrop of some sort. (A dark tablecloth draped over a box is fine.) Posing will highlight the item and illustrate its value better.

Finally, put the pictures and appraisal letters in a safety deposit box at your bank. Storing them in your home is like hiding Christmas gifts under your kids' beds.

● *Determine the Exclusions*

Review your policy to determine its exclusions. I live directly over the Midwest's New Madrid earthquake fault. In an informal survey of the homeowners in my neighborhood, I was the only one who had added earthquake coverage. There are homes far from any body of water which happen to be in flood plains. Normal insurance excludes such flood or earthquake coverage unless an additional rider is purchased. Find out what your policy includes and decide if you can live without it or if you are taking unnecessary chances by saving only a few dollars.

● *Review Your Liability Maximums*

Inflation has hit the courtrooms, too. Your liability coverage may be too small. Should the deliveryman slip on your child's toy and thereby end his career, can you afford it? In general, your liability coverage should be higher than in past years. It should also be the same as your other liability insurance. It doesn't make sense to carry $500,000 in liability coverage for your auto and carry only $200,000 for your home.

Both should be the higher amount if that's what you require.

● Shop Around for a Price

Prices vary greatly by carrier. Check with your lending institution to get their advice on carriers. With thousands of customers, the loan people deal with many carriers and should know what level of service they provide. Also write your state Board of Insurance for any cost comparison literature they provide. Most states publish comparative pricing booklets for the carriers operating within their borders.

● Raise Your Deductible

Your deductible limit, the amount you must pay before the insurance policy begins to reimburse, can greatly affect your premiums. My philosophy of home insurance is that I want to be guarded against catastrophe, not my neighbor's kid's bad throwing arm. Raising your deductible will often reduce premiums enough to pay the increase for replacement cost insurance or the natural disaster coverage currently excluded on your policy. This way your total premium is close to the same and your exposure to major loss is greatly reduced.

● Try Escrowing Your Own Insurance

In most states the lending institution accumulates your insurance premium monthly and makes the annual payment. Depending upon the state, you may not get interest on the amount collected and held each month. Ask the lending institution if you can't let them retain a copy of the policy and allow you to make your own payment once each year. This lets you earn the interest on your insurance payment amount.

● *Find a Good Agent*

As with any insurance purchase, your best bet is to deal with a good insurance agent. If your agent hasn't already mentioned some of these tips to you or called you for a year, then search for a new one. A good agent will be coming to you every so often with new ideas or suggestions about your coverage.

■ STORING WHAT YOU HAVE

Many people move to a bigger house when what they need are fewer useless and nonessential belongings. House junk and coat hangers have a lot in common. Every time you open the door, they seem to have been mating and raising families. What started out as a box in the corner of the basement ends up a pile of junk extending almost to the opposite wall. It's like a warped Parkinson's Law: "Junk expands to fill the space available to store it." Here's how to change your residence from a warehouse to a home.

Pretend you're going to move. Then ask yourself these questions about each item you review:

1. Who will use this?

2. How frequently will it be used?

3. When will it be used?

4. If I can't throw it out, how should it be stored?

Then follow these rules of good storage management:

○ *Store items near where they'll be used*

How many times have you heard someone say to you over the phone, "Can you hang on a minute while I go get a pen?" Storing your tools in the basement when they're used in the garage on the car is equally inefficient. When you work through your pretend move, check each item you keep for where it is used and store it nearby.

○ *Store items most frequently used in the most convenient places*

In the kitchen, for example, the most frequently used utensils should be in the handiest drawer. Clothing in the children's drawers or in your closets can be arranged by how often the items are worn rather than type of clothing. Or divide the kids' drawers by type of clothing, i.e., play, school, good, and dressy clothes, so you don't have to keep pawing through the drawers for a pair of play pants.

○ *Store items together if used together*

Broom and dustpan, pad and pencil, pans and stirrers, tar and feathers, and many more are used together and should be stored together. If you have to go to two places to accomplish one job, it's time for an IQ test.

○ *Return items to their place when finished with them*

I wish I could reclaim all the wasted seconds that I have spent looking for something I supposedly knew the location of. The motto around my house when I was growing up was, "Everything has a place and everything in its place," with a between-the-lines message—or else. It's either that, never find anything when you want it, or marry someone with ESP capabilities.

● *Utilize Wasted Space*

You can't realize how much space is available in living quarters until you take a tour past the Apollo capsule at the Smithsonian and peer into the interior. There isn't a cubic inch of wasted space. In the normal home a tremendous amount of storage space is wasted due to poor design or sloppy installation of shelving or closet rods. Some quick fixes for people overloaded with possessions or crammed into an apartment with limited storage space are:

○ *Use under-the-bed boxes*

These come with a zippered cover and pull-out handle for easy retrieval. You can store little-used or out-of-season items in them and free up an entire dresser or chest.

○ *Install a second-level closet rod*

Most hanging garments such as shirts, blouses, or folded pants reach only halfway to the floor. You can create twice as much rod space by simply adding a lower level rod much like the suit sales racks in a store. If you want something temporary, suspend another rod from the permanent one.

○ *Install a second-level closet shelf*

Most closet shelving is installed a little over five feet from the floor. In homes with the typical eight-foot ceilings, this leaves almost three feet of shelf space. Since it is difficult to stack objects three feet up due to irregular shapes and support problems, at least half the space between the shelf and ceiling is wasted. Install a second shelf midway and put little-used items up there.

○ *Add or install movable shelves*

Most kitchen cabinet arrangements waste nearly half their space. The distance between shelves is usually constant while the items stored vary in height. Glasses take up only about half the shelf space while stacks of plates use up all the space. Try to add shelves by varying the intershelf distance to fit the contents. It's not difficult to increase the total shelf capacity 20 to 30 percent.

○ *Use shelf and drawer organizers*

Hardware and department stores have a wide variety of shelf and drawer organizers to help you make better use of space. These include rotating units for deep cabinets, stackers for your china, bins for organizing drawers, under-cabinet drawer additions, and more.

○ *Install six-inch shelves*

One homeowner found herself short of kitchen pantry space. She converted a wall to storage by putting up six-inch-deep shelves floor to ceiling. The shelves were covered by sliding doors with wallpaper matching the breakfast area. The six inches of floor space were not missed and her pantry capacity was tripled at a small cost. This idea for keeping small items works anywhere floor space is tight.

● *Control What You Get*

Begin considering the cost of storage before you buy something. Set limits on what you will shove into the basement, garage, or closet. Try to reach a steady state where outgo equals income. Every time you pack something away, take the time to review what is already there and try to eliminate some of it.

Finally, buy multipurpose items. For example, there is the waffle iron, the grilled cheese plate, the hamburger cooker, the popcorn maker, etc. None of these separate appliances is necessary. Buy a food processor and use your pots and pans. Instead of three different types of game tables, use one. An all-weather goosedown jacket with a wide temperature comfort range can replace three coats and is a better buy. The list is nearly endless.

Remember, you manage your possessions or they will surely manage you. There's a pack rat latent in all of us. Keep sorting through life's accumulations and getting rid of what isn't necessary. Treat your home like a business treats a warehouse. Space costs money. Time spent getting something is wasted money. Organizing your possessions will earn you many precious seconds which can be spent doing something, anything, more interesting.

■ MINIMIZING YOUR ENERGY COSTS

Utilities costs are skyrocketing, which is reflected in rates. We have gone in a few short years from a country with no problem burning energy to a country with a burning energy problem. The energy shortage has begun to affect us where we are finally willing to take notice—in our pocketbooks.

There are lots of common ways to reduce energy costs. Here are a few of the simple ones you can do immediately.

● *Have Your Thermostat Adjusted*

It is estimated that as many as one third of all home thermostats are out of adjustment. Thermostats are sensitive and require careful adjustments at installation. Workmen often don't take the time to see that the thermostat is installed properly. If the on/off cycle temperature ranges are out of adjustment, the heater or air conditioner may start too soon and end too late. Also, the heat anticipator may not be matched to your furnace.

● *Get an Energy Audit*

Most power utilities offer a low-cost energy audit of your home either through the utility or by recommending an outside service. The audit entails an inspection of your home's construction and condition. The result is a list of suggestions to lower your utility bills. Some firms in cold weather areas even offer to provide detailed analysis of where your home is losing or leaking warm air. They utilize heat-sensitive infrared photography to identify exterior "hot spots" where warm air is leaking through. This can help you determine what should be done to seal your home.

● *Develop an Energy Miser Attitude*

Take care of the important home energy items. You might be carefully turning out the lights as you leave each room while a dripping faucet empties your hot water tank several times each week. Following is a checklist of simple energy savers:

1. Turn the heater pilot light off in summer
2. Convert outside gas lights to electricity
3. Enter and leave through a protected door (i.e., through the laundry room to the outside)
4. Turn water heater temperature to minimum acceptable (about 110 degrees)
5. Don't use the fireplace in very cold weather (it sucks heat up the chimney)
6. Check for adjustment in gas burners (blue flame only, no yellow)
7. Use stove-top gadgets instead of separate electric appliances (i.e., stove-top waffle iron or toaster)
8. Fix all dripping faucets (particularly the hot water)
9. Don't set the refrigerator too low (no frozen liquids in icebox side)
10. Let dishwasher air dry, run only full loads
11. Turn "instant on" TV feature off (it's always running)
12. Use fewer but higher watt light bulbs (two 75s gives less light than one 150)
13. Turn heater thermostat down if gone more than four hours (buy automatic timer to start back up before you return)
14. Paint rooms warm colors (red, orange, yellow make room feel warmer psychologically)

15. Turn off electric range burner early (residual coil heat will finish)
16. Use smallest burner for pan size on lowest setting practical (haste is waste)
17. Use glass or ceramic baking dishes (they retain heat better and allow you to reduce the setting 25 degrees)

These are the types of energy saving tips anyone can institute. All it takes is the miser spirit.

● **Seal Up Your Home**

In his book, *From the Walls In*, Charles Wing estimates how cold air gets into our homes:

Wall soleplate	25%
Wall outlets	20%
Windows	13%
Heating ductwork	13%
Bath, kitchen, dryer vents	10%
Doors	6%
Fireplace	6%
Miscellaneous	2%

The interesting fact from the chart is that the two most frequently sold energy remedies, storm windows and storm doors, help with only 19 percent of the problem. In all, the total inflow of cold air in the average home is equivalent to a four-square-foot window in the wall. It's tough trying to bring on springtime for the city with your home furnace.

To stop air coming in under the wall soleplate sitting on top of the home foundation, caulk around the soleplate. Electric sockets and switch boxes in the outside walls can be insulated by draft sealers which go under the faceplates. Caulking or weather-stripping windows, or adding an extra layer of air space with storm windows, has always improved window insulation. Heating ducts can be insulated with sheathing (as can hot water pipes). Vents can be taped shut where practical or weather-stripped for a tighter fit.

Doors allow the greatest loss of heat from opening and closing in winter. Weather-stripping and sealing the door is the first step. A storm door won't be of much extra value unless the storm door can be closed before opening the inside door, creating a protected door.

Finally, unless you own one of the forced air fireplace grates which circulate heated air back into the room, the fireplace is an energy USER rather than saver. Also, when the fire goes out overnight, the open flue lets cold air down the chimney into the house. A glass fireplace screen which closes will help minimize this overnight infiltration of air.

It doesn't take more than a weekend or so to seal up your house and reduce the size of that four-square-foot window in the side of your home. Then adopting the miser mentality will help you minimize what is used inside.

● *Getting Through to the Power Utilities*

For both electric and gas utilities, Mondays are the worst days. Noontime is also busy, as workers call in about billing problems during their lunch hour. For the electric companies, summertime is three to four times as busy as winter due to high bill complaints. The exact opposite is true with the gas company.

● *Think Twice About the Level Payment Plan*

Most power companies offer an alternative billing scheme for customers objecting to the seasonality of their bills. Called "budget billing" or some other variance, it lets the customer pay an even amount each month instead of paying high bills during the heavy usage months and low bills in the light usage season. There are several drawbacks to this plan you should consider.

The utility turns a tidy profit on this "convenience." The fixed monthly amount is calculated by taking the total yearly anticipated bill and dividing by 11, not 12. The utility then sells the benefit of having a small final bill the twelfth month. What's good for the utility is that you are actually prepaying your bill a small amount each month. While it's not a big deal to you, multiplied by hundreds of thousands of customers, the prepayments add up to a sizeable chunk of interest-free money to the utility in a time of soaring prime lending rates.

■ HOME MAINTENANCE

With the housing industry in such a sorry state in recent years, the home improvement business is expanding. With the trend, there has been increased attention on fraudulent services. A new widow told me of being called by a "home improvement specialist" who had passed by her house and "noticed a real problem." Her chimney was cracked, she was told, and needed tuck-pointing. The only problem was that her frame house had no chimney.

Follow this simple list when dealing with any home improvement firm:

1. Find out how long they've been in business. The longer the better.

2. Find out if they have a permanent mailing address and phone number. Avoid P.O. boxes or companies not listed in the white or Yellow Pages.

3. Find out if they are properly licensed as a contractor or business in your city, county, or state. If they are incorporated, they must file with the Secretary of State. If you have questions, contact that office.

4. Find out if you get a WRITTEN warranty of materials and workmanship. If it isn't in writing, it never happened.

5. Find out if they have a list of satisfied customers you can call. If it's a long list, call several at the top, middle, and bottom. Operators have been known to salt the top of the list with friends, knowing most people won't call more than two or three people.

6. Find out if the Better Business Bureau has anything on them.

7. Don't sign a thing until you've had a chance to think about it. If they rush you, turn them away.

8. Finally, if it's a large contract, tell them you'll meet them in their office to sign. If they object, tell them to get lost. Once there, take a last look around and see if this is the type of operation you want to give several thousand dollars.

● *Get an Hour's Work for an Hour's Pay*

One of my pet peeves is servicemen who charge an hour minimum for labor and fix the problem in ten minutes. One person told me he parked his car behind the service truck and made the repairman stay the other fifty minutes since he was paying for it anyway. I don't want to get into a beef with a repairman. Instead, see if there is anything else he could do for you in the remaining hour. It's a great opportunity to get miscellaneous items adjusted or repaired at no additional cost.

■ TAKING CARE OF YOUR PLANT LIFE

You read what I think about growing things in Chapter 1. The only growing green thing I really like is the Incredible Hulk. So here are a few tips on getting that wonderful mediocre look with the least amount of effort.

● *Plant a Zoysia Yard*

Nothing is more beautiful than the luxurious green Kentucky bluegrass yard featured on the front of every bag of Scott's fertilizer. I know zoysia grass greens up late and browns early with the first frost. But it requires so little maintenance! I love a lawn that refuses to let the bad guys grow all by itself. It spreads on its own accord and chokes everything else out. If you stand on a zoysia lawn too long, it throws you off. That's my kind of yard.

● *Rent Out Your Yard*

One working woman has solved the yard problem in back. She rents out her backyard to the neighbors in return for some of the products they grow. She doesn't have anything to mow, the neighbors take loving care of her backyard, and she gets free produce.

● *Grow Indoor Plants You Can Ignore*

With my brown thumb, I need green stuff that grows in spite of me. Indoors, raise plants that don't require much care. Cacti are ideal plants, as are certain palms. Ivy isn't too greedy about care. Other good plants are schefflera and the stripe-leaf dracaena. If you aren't a corporate farmer or have sons named Hoss and Little Joe, ask your local nursery folks about what plants will thrive on indifference.

■ BUYING A HOME

At the time this is written, it is easier to run for President than obtain a home loan. If the Federal Reserve has put a clamp on loan funds, then there is little you can do. But assuming that someday the financial community will let us again buy homes, here are some tips.

● *Use All Your Connections to Obtain Money*

This is when it pays to have connections. If you haven't been cultivating your banker or savings and loan officer (more about this in Chapter 5), then you must count on others. If you work for a large company, have someone from the finance department call the company's bank in your behalf. A word from a multimillion dollar depositor carries a bit more weight than just another loan application among thousands.

Naturally, all the people involved in the sale will be eager to help with your loan. The broker, the local lending firm the builder uses, the seller's mortgage holder, and the real estate firms can also pull a few strings. Many times the mortgage holder of a used house is happy to assist since it allows the institution to collect prepayment penalties on the sale and to convert an older loan to current higher interest levels. The sale is a money-maker for the institution.

● *Swap Investment or Business Property*

If you have investment property or business equipment and you wish to invest it elsewhere, you can postpone gains taxes under certain conditions. You will want to see a lawyer or tax expert on the details. Just be aware that you don't necessarily have to sell property outright in all cases.

● *Use a Private Mortgage Insurer (If Needed)*

Mortgage insurance allows you to buy a home with a lower down payment than would normally be required. Should you default on the mortgage, the insurer would then cover any loss the lending institution would incur in selling your home, a less than tender thought. A good way to obtain mortgage insurance is to utilize one of the private companies such as MGIC (Mortgage Guarantee Insurance Corporation) or GEMIC (General Electric Mortgage Insurance Corporation). The private companies usually have lower premiums than the FHA or VA and require less paper work. Service also is much faster. Applications are handled in days instead of ice ages.

If you have some type of private mortgage insurance, be aware that it should run only for the life of the risk, *not the life of the loan.* Only 20 to 25 percent of the total loan is insured at a cost of 1/4 of one percent on your loan. When you have repaid that much of the loan, you should request the lending institution discontinue coverage, thereby lowering your monthly payment. For example, with a $70,000 loan over thirty years, reducing the interest from 10 percent to 9 3/4 percent lowers the payment $12.90 monthly. Most lenders are happy to do this. The trick is YOU MUST ASK FOR IT. The lender will not initiate the reduction when you qualify. They are happy to let you keep paying the insurance forever in ignorance. Their investment is that much safer.

● *Inspect the Home*

If you see a home that fits your needs and you wish to buy, make this short inspection:

○ *Check the basement for water damage*

A good sign is papers or cardboard boxes on the floor. If there is water leakage, these will be off the ground, and the basement will look like a stilt city.

○ *Check the age of the furnace*

Aluminum forced-air furnaces have an average life of fifteen years. Also, find out the age of the air-conditioning unit. Depending upon the type, it may also be ready to meet its Maker (or His repairman).

○ *Check the structural stability*

Watch out for sloping floors or cracked door-frames. Doorframes are particularly susceptible to cracking when there is movement.

○ *Check the plumbing*

Try every faucet. If the water comes out nice and brown, there is probably corrosion. In a bathroom, turn on the tub and sink faucet and then flush the toilet. This will give you an indicator of water pressure.

○ *Check the attic*

Get a flashlight and look up in the attic. You can't tell how much insulation is in the walls, but you can see the thickness up above. Look for water marks on the wood from leaks.

○ *Ask to see the actual utility bills*

Don't accept a prepared sheet; examine the stubs. This house may allow you to heat half the neighborhood.

○ *Talk to the neighbors*

Do a little investigative work with the neighbors. If they lie to you, they risk having problems with you when you move in. Talk about the schools, the builder, the snow service, the garbage pickup, nearby sinkholes—all those invisible items that can make an area livable.

○ *Call in a qualified inspection engineer*

If the house passes all the above tests, go ahead and call in an engineer specializing in home inspections. You'll be spending in the area of $100 to protect a six figure investment. Buying a home without a professional inspection is nothing more than realty Russian roulette.

■ RATING A HOME FOR LIVABILITY

Most of us had the displeasure of moving into a beautiful home and finding out certain parts of it were unlivable due to poor design or a mismatch with our furniture. It's difficult to walk through an apartment or house and accurately picture what it will be like to live there. It's similar to rearranging furniture. You don't know how it will look until you move it.

Pat Hilderbrand, Assistant Professor in the Department of Housing and Interior Design at the University of Missouri–Columbia, has developed a list of rules and space guides to use when purchasing or designing a new home:

● *Avoid Major Traffic Ways Through Rooms*

If you can help it, you don't want to go through the living room to get to the kitchen or through the family room to get to the garage. Rooms stay neater and cleaner, and you avoid wearing paths in carpeting. Traffic through an activity area, such as children walking through a conversation in the living room to get snacks in the kitchen turn a room into a parade ground.

● *Place Buffers Between Quiet and Noisier Areas*

Nothing is more frustrating than getting friendly in the master bedroom and hearing the guests in the next room coughing. Or being kept up by a noisy party when the family room is next to a bedroom. Some type of buffer, a room, a bathroom, or a closet, separates areas best for sleeping and studying or for privacy. Think about the placement of rooms and the furniture within rooms that maximize your buffer areas.

● *Avoid a Bathroom Adjacent to Entertaining Areas*

We all laughed each time Archie Bunker went stomping upstairs to be followed by a distinctive "FFFLLLUUUSSSHHH." When the flushing noise is quite obvious, many people are embarrassed. This is a social disruption you can eliminate with proper layout. Keep the door out of sight of the living areas, too. This will save your guests the embarrassment of being watched entering and leaving the bathroom.

● *Have a Private Hall*

It's good to have the bedroom hall out of view of the living area. This makes the bedroom area more private. Children or other family members can go from a bedroom to a bathroom in tattered jammies without entertaining those in the living area.

● *Avoid a Long Closet on an Outside Wall*

Unless there is a heating or cooling duct in the closet, you will be constantly climbing into ice-cube cold clothes in winter and toasty warm clothes in summer. (The only advantage is that the closet provides a small amount of extra insulation to the exterior wall and may keep the room slightly more comfortable.)

● *Check the Location of Wall Outlets and Switches*

Most newer homes have one or two receptacles on each wall. Older homes may have fewer outlets than needed, which turns the home into a booby trap of lamp-cord trip-wires. Also determine which outlet the wall switches control. These are often designed by madmen. The socket you plug your lamp into is constantly on, while a socket behind the door where nothing can be put is controlled at the door switch. If you're having a home built, specify which outlet you want controlled by the door switch.

■ THE EFFICIENT KITCHEN

A carefully designed kitchen can save many hours of food preparation time and eliminate much effort. A poor one can make you want to eat the kitchen instead of the food. Fortunately the same principles that industrial engineers have used to design assembly lines can be applied to the home. Rose E. Steidl, Professor Emeritus of the Department of Design and Environmental Analysis at Cornell University, an expert on design factors and productivity in the home, is the author of Cornell Extension Bulletin NE 241, *Functional Kitchens*. In it she details a number of design considerations in making food preparation easier:

● *Have Your Workplace at the Right Height*

The height of counters and tabletops in the kitchen depends upon your body, your vision, and the type of work you will be doing. The standard countertop is 36 inches high. Depending upon your physique, this could be too high or too low. If it is high, you will feel like a Munchkin. If it is too low, you will become the Hunchback of Notre-Dame.

Kitchen countertops should have two levels to match the two types of food preparation tasks. You can calculate these by first determining your elbow height. Have someone measure from the floor to the bottom of your arm when the elbow is at your side and your forearm is parallel with the floor. This figure is the basis for all calculations.

The higher counter is used to perform regular kitchen jobs which require no leverage, such as dishing out food or doing light cutting. This counter should be approximately 3 inches lower than your elbow for comfort. For example, if you are tall and your elbow height is 42 inches, the typical counter is 3 inches too short for you when doing most common kitchen chores. The lower counter is for jobs which require leverage such as carving, or require the use of some appliance like a mixer. This counter should be 6 to 7 inches below your elbow. In the example, the average counter would be fine for these jobs.

If your kitchen counter is too low for everyday jobs, you might want to invest in a large block to give you some elevated space. If the counter is too high, you can obtain a cutting block table for those heavy leverage jobs. If all else fails, women can wear comfortable heels or flats for kitchen work, depending upon whether they need to be taller or shorter. If you are building a home, make certain you have counter space at both heights.

As a side note, most sinks and ovens are at the wrong height. Since sinks are installed at counter height, and most sink work is done about 1 inch from the bottom of the sink, they are too low. Make certain your sink is mounted in the higher counter portion, i.e., about 2 or 3 inches below your elbow. The wall-mounted oven should be installed so that the open door is 1 to 7 inches below your elbow. (Average preference is about 3 inches below.) This is not only a good height for lifting out heavy dishes, but having the open door below your elbow will save you nasty burns on reaching in. The over-under microwave oven combination cleverly has both at the wrong heights. The microwave above is too high and the oven below is too low so that you have to stoop. The only alternative is to put them side-by-side or on separate walls.

● *Keep the Front Sink Barrier Narrow*

Another design flaw is to install the sink too far from the countertop edge. This puts the sink work too far out from your body causing you to bend slightly, a posture more suitable to the lead in *Planet of the Apes*. The sink barrier rim should be no more than 3 inches wide to keep the work close.

● *Locate Kitchen Centers to Match Your Work Flow*

You can implement the following tips:

1. Place the sink and range close together. The most trips are made between these two centers, so this will save many steps. Of the two, the sink center is used the most. Give it the best location.

2. Place the dishwasher near the dish storage. Whether the dishwasher is to the left or right of the sink depends upon your personal habits, handedness, and the location of your cabinet space. Hopefully your dishes will be stored near the serving center, so the dishwasher might best go between the sink and serving center.

3. Store china near the table or dishwasher. This will save steps when setting the table and serving food, and when putting away clean dishes.

4. Keep a separate freezer out of the work flow. Locate it at one end of the kitchen or in another part of the house. It is only used periodically and creates more space between important work centers.

● *Have Enough Electrical Outlets*

When you have a radio, can opener, toaster, TV, food processor, and whatever else regularly sitting on the countertop, then add a mixer and an electric knife, suddenly electrical outlets are at a premium. Count the number of appliances you may have running at one time and then make certain your kitchen has enough sockets to handle them without overloading a single outlet.

● *Own a Dishwasher*

As a child I did dishes nearly every meal in what I thought was a horrible violation of the child labor laws. If you count up the hours you spend each week washing and drying dishes, you will quickly see that a dishwasher costs less than a dollar per hour saved within the first year of use. After years of service, the final tally is pennies per hour of kitchen time saved. If you don't yet have a dishwasher, pummel somebody without mercy until you get one.

■ COOKING FASTER AND EASIER

Not only can you speed up the meal preparation process by having an efficient kitchen, you can reduce the overall amount of work that needs to be done. For example:

● *Delegate*

The next time one of your genetic experiments wanders in to complain about the lack of food on the table, delegate. I'm amazed at the number of friends who are working away in the kitchen while the kids (or spouse) are wasting away in front of the TV. God didn't write a job description saying the cook is the only one who can set the table and serve up food. Let the screaming Mongolian horde earn its keep.

● *Don't Get Fancy*

Whether a plain dinner or formal entertaining, don't let your ego get in the way of your judgment. Stick to no more than one or two fancy dishes per meal. Good food will never take a back seat to fancy food. Make it easy on yourself.

● *Minimize Food Choices*

Plan the meal so that you serve second helpings rather than a wide variety of food. You don't need three vegetables, two potatoes, and several salads. Take a tip from restaurant professionals handling heavy crowds, such as on New Year's Eve, and limit your menu.

● *Prepare in Advance*

With multiple-oven kitchens and microwave technology, it's much easier now to prepare most of a meal in advance and then heat things up right before serving time. Even for the week's lunches, batch them all up and defrost the food daily as needed. Just remember to store the food in its most usable form. For example, have the vegetable in its serving dish before storing. Then merely pop it into the microwave or whatever and it will be ready to serve immediately when done.

● *Use Heat Spikes*

A truly clever product that isn't used as much as it should be is the heat spike. Conventional cooking time can be reduced by as much as 50 percent with heat spikes. The nail-shaped hollow spikes, when inserted into meat or potatoes for example, help to distribute the inside heat faster and more evenly. In this way, meat cooks inside and outside (instead of outside-in) while retaining size and important juices.

● *Microwave Cooking*

This is another modern household appliance no kitchen should be without. You haven't lived until you've stumbled foggily down the stairs for the two o'clock feeding, slopped that horrible-smelling formula into those narrow-necked bottles, and then heated a pan of water with the bottle in it. All this takes place to the tune of a screaming baby. Then you either permanently scar your wrist because the bottle is too hot, or the baby spits the nipple out in disgust because the milk is too cold. Well, no more.

The first application of our microwave was the night feeding bottle. Pop the bottle from the refrigerator to the microwave and thirty-five seconds later is a perfectly warmed meal for a ravenous mouth. Cold coffee is turned into a steaming cup in sixty seconds. Restaurant service as good as this is hard to find.

Now using a microwave is hardly anything new or a special tip. As St. Louis radio personality Jack Carney said during our interview, "If one more author comes on this show hyping her microwave

book, I'm going to stuff her in it and set it on high."
Yet microwaves can help you when there is no other
way out: you forgot to take the meat out of the
freezer, you got home too late to start the roast, the
turkey is cooking too slowly and dinner will be
delayed, etc.

Below are selected entries from a mid-70s study by
Thermador/Waste King, Inc. listing the cooking time
for common dishes:

Dish	Oven Time	Microwave Time
Baked Beans (serves 4)	60 minutes	10 minutes
Upside-Down Cake (1 box mix)	57 minutes*	8 minutes
Pork Loin Roast (4 lbs.)	225 minutes	57 minutes
Rare Rump Roast (4 lbs.)	136 minutes*	23 minutes
Turkey (12 lbs., 9 oz.)	287 minutes	78 minutes**
TV Dinner (15 oz.)	28 minutes	9½ minutes

*Includes preheat time
**Includes browning element time

Overall, for all foods included in the study, the
microwave oven saved over 70 percent of the cooking time and over 60 percent of the kilowatt hours

used. Like so many worthwhile household appliances, a microwave will cost very little for each hour of time it saves you.

So view your home like any good business views its place of work and minimize operational costs of both time and money.

"Traveler: A person of long standing."
                                    –Anonymous

4

Travel: Getting There Faster

Whoever said, "Getting there is half the fun," was looking forward to a miserable second half of the trip. Even under the best of circumstances, travel is one hassle after another. Yet most people feel we're much better off than our ancestors whose prairie schooners rumbled across the country for months. Common wisdom says we have it much easier with air travel, superhighways, and billion-dollar commuter systems toiling away underground.

But in some situations travel has become even *more difficult* as it has speeded up. I'd like to wheel Ward Bond and his wagon train up to Chicago's O'Hare the Wednesday evening before Thanksgiving and see how the hardy pioneers fare. I'd like them to roll along an L.A. freeway at 5:00 P.M. and see how far their oxen get. I'd like them to grab their backpacks and see if they saunter through New York's subway system at 5:15. Easier? I don't think wagon trains faced survival tests any rougher than the congestion of modern travel.

While *travel time*, the actual time spent going from place to place, does keep decreasing (some argue that we can actually travel faster than we *want* to with the Concorde SST), TIME SPENT TRAVELING is still the key measurement. And though there are no Indians to threaten the modern travelers, dangers still exist. Instead of a broken axle or an arrow in the back, there are traffic jams, endless flight delays, and lost luggage.

In this chapter I can't promise to speed up your travel time—and make your journey more pleasant—in all cases. But the tips here will reduce the total *time spent traveling* and make your trips proceed more quickly and easily.

■ TRAVEL AGENTS

The travel agency industry is growing right along with the airlines. There are about 13,000 agencies taking advantage of the fact that tourism, at $360 billion per year, is the world's second largest industry behind petroleum. Best of all, travel agent services are FREE to you since their income is from commissions paid by airlines, hotels, tours, etc.

● *Use an Out-of-the-Way Agent*

Find a travel agent with an office out of the general flow of shopping traffic. Department store agents draw too many one-shot clients. You want an agent who exists only through repeat business as a result of good service.

● *Look for the ASTA Emblem*

Use a member of the American Society of Travel Agents. There are no guarantees here, but the ASTA requires its members be professionally trained and financially sound.

● *Look for Computer Terminals*

Many of the better travel agents tie into one of the major airline computer reservations systems. This means the agent doesn't have to phone various airlines for availability or quotes. When you are in a pinch calling long distance, this can be critical in making a flight.

● *Avoid Busy Times*

The worst time for travel agents is October and November as people make their Christmas plans. Rainy and snowy winter days are also unusually busy because desperate people call up demanding, "Get me out of here! I can't stand it anymore." Monday and Friday are the busy days of the week.

■ **AIRLINE TRAVEL**

With the rapid growth of airline travel, problems are inevitable. Airlines are gobbling each other faster than Jaws can sample swimmers. With all the expansion to new routes and cities, with new combinations and fares, delays are inevitable. Don't think, though, that the passenger is the only one worried about excessive delays. In 1977, the last year for which complete statistics are available, delays caused U.S. airlines to burn an additional 700 million gallons of fuel—over 8 percent of their total usage. Delays not only inconvenienced passengers by detaining them some 60 million hours, delays cost the airlines over $800 million. The experienced air traveler knows there are a great number of simple procedures to save time.

Rank	City	ID	Passengers in Thousands
1	Chicago O'Hare	ORD	21,119
2	Atlanta Midfield	ATL	20,720
3	Los Angeles International	LAX	15,003
4	Dallas—Ft. Worth Regional	DFW	10,609
5	San Francisco International	SFO	10,442
6	Denver Stapleton	DEN	9,851
7	New York John F. Kennedy	JFK	9,205
8	New York LaGuardia	LGA	8,778
9	Miami International	MIA	8,118
10	Boston Logan	BOS	7,075
11	Washington National	DCA	6,935
12	Honolulu International	HNL	5,686
13	Pittsburgh International	PIT	5,450
14	St. Louis Lambert International	STL	5,423
15	Detroit Metropolitan-Wayne County	DTW	5,224
16	Houston Intercontinental	IAH	5,036
17	Las Vegas McCarran	LAS	4,838
18	Seattle Tacoma International	SEA	4,561
19	Minneapolis-St. Paul International	MSP	4,553
20	Newark International	EWR	4,427
21	Philadelphia International	PHL	4,350
22	Tampa International	TPA	3,738
23	Cleveland Hopkins	CLE	3,571
24	Phoenix Sky Harbor International	PHX	3,449
25	Orlando International	MCO	3,225

25 BUSIEST U.S. AIRPORTS
(CAB statistics for 12-month period ending June 1980).
TABLE 4-1

● *Fly Through Smaller Airports*

The major reason for delay is overcrowding at the airports. Approximately 65 percent of all passengers in the U.S. board at just twenty-five of the 14,500 U.S. airports. The twenty-five major airports shown in Table 4-1 are the sites of 75 percent of all delays.

During peak hours and days, these airports simply have more traffic than they can handle. When booking a flight, go through the lesser used airports. For example, when flying from St. Louis to Toronto, I have the choice of connecting through Chicago, Detroit, Pittsburgh, Minneapolis, or Cleveland. Chicago is a nightmare anytime. I've found that my best route is connecting through Cleveland because this seems to generate the fewest delays.

When in doubt, use the "receiver" airport of a large city. Examples are Chicago's Midway or Dallas's Love Field. These tend to be closer to business centers and cause even fewer delays.

● *Avoid Rush Hour Departures*

Flying off peak can help dramatically. Monday through Thursday are the best days for travel—Friday the worst. A flight around 5:00 P.M. any day will cause delays because of the heavy schedule for business people. The only off-peak time to avoid is the last flight on a day's schedule. Carriers rarely cancel rush hour flights but are not as hesitant about scrubbing near-empty late flights when the few passengers can be shifted to another airline.

● *Pick the Shortest Air Time*

Pay attention to times quoted when making a reservation. Calculate the actual travel time across the time zones. You may have been booked on a puddle jumper landing at every red light. Also, intermediate landings increase the chance of being delayed or canceled due to mechanical problems.

Even on a nonstop flight, compare air times between flights and carriers. For example, the scheduled direct flights from New York to Los Angeles currently vary from 5 hours and 25 minutes to 5 hours and 57 minutes, a 32-minute difference. Flights from New York to St. Louis show an 18-minute variance. Generally, you may be able to cut as much as 10 percent of the flight time by picking the best alternative.

● *Choose Your Airline for Service*

The Civil Aeronautics Board (CAB) publishes a monthly summary of consumer complaints by cause and by airline. While the CAB is careful to point out that the volume of customer complaints should not be used to rate airlines, any prudent traveler can draw interesting conclusions. As an illustration, in September 1980 the number of complaints per 100,000 boardings varied from 12.09 for Pan Am to 1.43 for Delta. It's tough to ignore an 8 to 1 difference in complaint volumes.

The figures in Table 4-2 will be out of date by the time you read this. If you travel frequently and wish to keep track of airline performance, you or your travel agent should get on the CAB mailing list for consumer bulletins. Address your request to: CAB, Bureau of Compliance and Consumer Protection, Washington, D.C. 20428.

Airline	Complaints per 100,000 Passengers
Pan American	12.09
TWA	9.80
Texas International	9.78
Braniff	6.59
American	5.17
Eastern	4.12
Continental	3.96
Republic	3.83
USAIR	3.68
Frontier	3.33
Ozark	3.01
United	2.95
Delta	1.43

COMPLAINTS FOR SELECTED DOMESTIC AIRLINES IN SEPTEMBER 1980 (from CAB statistics). TABLE 4-2

● *How to Get Tickets*

The worst place to do anything is the airport. Parking is horrible, lines are outrageous, and the counters are so far apart only a dedicated marathoner can make connections without a heart seizure. Here are the best alternatives:

○ *Travel agent*

Let the agent sort through the carriers, schedules, and fare options. A single phone call is all it takes. You can then go in and pick up the tickets or have them mailed to you. If there is a refund or other special needs, the agent takes care of that, too.

○ *City office*

Since many airports are located a short rocket trip from the metropolitan hub, most airlines maintain a ticket office in the center of the business district. If this is near where you live or work, you can do your face-to-face planning here.

○ *Join an airline club*

This is the best place to change tickets at the airport. There is a membership fee, but you do gain access to a truly relaxing place to wait and conduct business at the airport if need be.

● *Tell the Airline Exactly What You Need*

When you make reservations, let the booking agent know your special requirements. Airlines offer as many as ten special meals: religious, dietetic, vegetarian, low salt, low carbohydrate, low sodium, bland, etc. You can even advance order special meals such as a seafood plate if you travel the same flight regularly and want a change from the normal dog food. You can even request special handling. I traveled nursing a broken ankle once and was chauffeured, rolled, and helped from point to point by solicitous airline personnel.

● *Check Your Tickets*

Although the computer or agent rarely makes mistakes, I've been given tickets where flight numbers or times were incorrect. Also remember to treat your tickets as cash. They are negotiable and can be cashed in for new tickets or money.

● Ask About Price Increases

My travel agent knows to bill me directly before a trip when I pick up the tickets. Sometimes I get a call telling me about a price increase before I depart. I then have the option of paying early at the old price or holding on to my money until departure. Last year ticket prices increased at least once per month (and often twice per month). Travelers making reservations months in advance went to pay for their tickets and absorbed a 20 percent or more price increase. Just remember that a reservation doesn't guarantee a price; only money changing hands does that.

● Pack to Carry On All Bags

Richard Pascarelli suggested an excellent way to get rid of nuclear waste in an *OMNI* article: "Put it in little suitcases and check it with the airlines—we'll never see it again." The airline can't lose what it never touched. Carry your luggage on or don't bring it. Normally you may carry on one underseat bag and one hanging suit bag. Some airlines also have special overhead or forward luggage compartments for bigger bags. Keeping my belongings with me has saved me from not having to track down my bags when changing flights at the last minute literally hundreds of times.

If you must check baggage because of your safari mentality, at least carry on all essential toiletries and medicines along with several days' change of clothes.

If your baggage disappears into another dimension you can still go on with your trip.

● *Use Hard Baggage*

Own the hard molded luggage with a combination lock. The beautiful, light, soft luggage can be split down the side in seconds, rifled, and then retaped from the inside so that you never notice until you want to capture that haunting picture. You open your bag. Oops. Your camera is gone. Sorry.

● *Never Put Your Home Address on the Name Tag*

Name tags are a real service to thieves who otherwise would have to track down empty homes. Airport burglary rings get your name off the tag and strip your home while you are away. Put your *business* address and phone on the tag and also IN THE BAG in case the tag is lost.

● *Write Down What You Are Taking and Leave the*
   List at Home (or Carry It)

If for some reason your belongings disappear into the friendly skies forever, you will need to know *exactly* what you lost. The airlines currently allow a maximum of $750 per bag. This sounds okay except that you are paid on the *depreciated* value of your muumuus and other treasures. So not only do you need to know the original cost of each item, you need to list its age.

If $750 isn't enough to cover your belongings (and it isn't much, considering today's cost of clothing), you may want to purchase additional insurance. The extra coverage costs only about 10 cents per $100 value. If anyone knows how to get a damage claim paid quickly, let me know. Normally, if you file a claim you are locked into the computer backlog for several months.

● *Call Before You Leave for the Airport*

Call the day you leave to get the status of your flight. You don't want to arrive only to find out your flight has been canceled. You see, O. J. Simpson flies through airports because his airplane has been grounded. Find out if the times are still valid. Schedules change and you may not have been notified. I once showed up for a flight with an out-of-date ticket only to find out the flight left two hours earlier each day since the start of the month. If the flight has been canceled, you can reschedule at home instead of joining the other lemmings in their rush to the sea.

● *Find Out If the Flight Is Overbooked*

Those clever airline people have found out that we passengers are not very trustworthy. We make reservations and then sometimes don't keep them. Of course, occasionally we fool them and all show up. This isn't a problem unless the greedy airline has been counting on our untrustworthiness and sold more tickets than it has seats. This is called "overbooking." When that happens, first come, first served. Find out if your flight is overbooked when you call before leaving for the airport. Then you'll know how early you had better be at the gate. An hour will usually suffice to guarantee you a seat.

● *Always Carry a Roll of Dimes*

The humble telephone is your best buddy when the airport system begins to turn hostile. Nothing is more pitiful than seeing a $100,000-a-year executive begging strangers or bargaining with the Hare Krishnas to get change for the phone.

● *Double-check the Skycap*

The check-in step at the airport used to be a simple procedure of walking up to the proper counter agent and handing over your ticket and bags (if any). Many airports now have curbside check-in where you give your bags to the skycap and he tags them and sends them on their way. Save time by having your ticket ready. He won't tag your bag without it. Otherwise you could turn in your bag, have a friend claim it, and end up with free shipping.

Watch the skycap carefully to make certain you get the right number of stubs and the correct stubs back. Also look at the symbol he writes on the tag. You will see something like: LGA, LAX, ORD, CDA, etc. These are the airport symbols. (Symbols for the top twenty-five airports are in Table 4-1.) Make certain your bags are carrying the right tags and symbols. I've seen skycaps handling several groups at once get all the people, bags, and stubs mixed up.

● *Check In with Care*

Don't take just any seat in the appropriate section. The rows over the wing give the smoothest ride, while the seats up front are quietest. You haven't lived until you've sat in the rear of a DC-9 "vibra-jet" between the engines. (I swear the pilots purposely get the engines just out of sync to give the traveler that brain-numbing "rhun, rhun, rhun . . ." resonance.)

If you are right-handed, you may prefer the left aisle seat for a meal flight so that you will have elbow room and vice versa for left-handers. Stay away from seats near the galleys. They are very noisy and are usually last on the meal serving order.

Ask the agent how full the flight is. If it isn't sold out, request a row with an empty middle seat. He can't guarantee it will stay empty, but other people behind you will choose middle seats last. You may have it empty for your flight.

In general, you are better off sitting in the front of your section. From a time standpoint, nonsmoking rows are better than smoking rows because the planes empty front to back. Avoid bulkhead rows. Most families with small children travel here. It's no fun doing your jungle gym imitation while some strange kid drools all over your Johnny Carson suit or Saks outfit.

● *Getting Back in the Air When Your Flight Is Canceled*

So far the air travel tips have been fairly straightforward with a few simple tricks to speed you on your way. Where you truly need to be an insider is when the carefully scheduled air travel system begins to unravel. Flights are so interdependent that a single major airport closing due to bad weather can affect the whole country.

○ *Never go with the herd*

When a flight is canceled, the gate agent will direct you to go to the main terminal ticket counter to be booked on another flight. The angry elephant herd trumpets and stampedes down the concourse fighting to be first in line. This is the WORST place to go. The airline service representative sees the angry throng approaching with mutters of mutiny and throws a few more ticket agents into the fray. They climb on the terminals, block-book other flights, and start parceling out reservations. This procedure is something akin to a run on a failing bank.

○ *Call your travel agent (even long distance)*

If it is normal business hours, pull out your trusty roll of dimes and call your travel agent collect. They are happy to accept charges and bill you later. Explain your problem and tell them what you need. They can climb on their terminal (or call on their special lines) and book you within a few minutes. You will have your new flight before the herd even reaches the terminal desk. What you must do now is beat the block-booking done by the ticket agent when the crowd arrives. Call the carrier you now have and find out the gate. If that information isn't available over the phone, ask a gate agent which concourse the carrier uses. Then you can go directly to the concourse and find the gate without having to return to the main terminal. (Hint: This only works if you are carrying everything on. See what I meant?)

○ *Borrow an OAG and reschedule yourself*

If your travel agent is closed, then you must do your own reservations work. Go to the nearest desk of any airlines and ask to see their OAG (Official Airlines Guide). An OAG lists the complete airlines schedule. (Have your travel agent show you how to

HOW TO USE THE POCKET FLIGHT GUIDE

The Pocket Flight Guide contains quick reference airline schedules for the top 48 U.S. and 5 Canadian traffic producing cities. The other cities included are based on a minimum passenger volume between them and each of these 53 cities. **Schedules appearing in this publication represent all nonstop and one-stop flights and supplementary multi-stop flights between the origin and destination cities shown.**

Destination cities are listed in alphabetical order. Reservations telephone numbers for airlines whose schedules appear in this Guide are published immediately following the schedule listings. New users should study the sample listing below to familiarize themselves with the information shown:

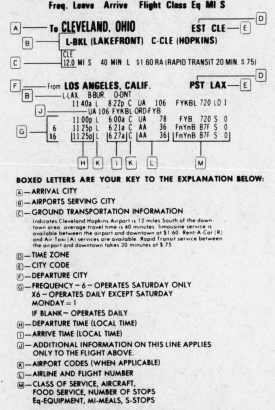

BOXED LETTERS ARE YOUR KEY TO THE EXPLANATION BELOW:

Ⓐ — ARRIVAL CITY

Ⓑ — AIRPORTS SERVING CITY

Ⓒ — GROUND TRANSPORTATION INFORMATION

    Indicates Cleveland Hopkins Airport is 12 miles South of the downtown area. average travel time is 40 minutes. limousine service is available between the airport and downtown at $1.60. Rent-A-Car (R) and Air-Taxi (A) services are available. Rapid Transit service between the airport and downtown takes 20 minutes at $.75.

Ⓓ — TIME ZONE

Ⓔ — CITY CODE

Ⓕ — DEPARTURE CITY

Ⓖ — FREQUENCY – 6 – OPERATES SATURDAY ONLY

    X6 – OPERATES DAILY EXCEPT SATURDAY

    MONDAY = 1

    IF BLANK – OPERATES DAILY

Ⓗ — DEPARTURE TIME (LOCAL TIME)

Ⓘ — ARRIVE TIME (LOCAL TIME)

Ⓙ — ADDITIONAL INFORMATION ON THIS LINE APPLIES ONLY TO THE FLIGHT ABOVE.

Ⓚ — AIRPORT CODES (WHEN APPLICABLE)

Ⓛ — AIRLINE AND FLIGHT NUMBER

Ⓜ — CLASS OF SERVICE, AIRCRAFT, FOOD SERVICE, NUMBER OF STOPS

    Eq-EQUIPMENT, MI-MEALS, S-STOPS

See Abbreviations and Reference Marks pages 4 and 5 for explanation of codes and abbreviations used in this issue.

TABLE 4-3

POCKET FLIGHT GUIDE

To ST. LOUIS, MO.					CST STL		To ST. LOUIS, MO.					CST STL	

From KANSAS CITY, MO.-CONT.   MKC

X6	5.30p C	6.26p I	TW	546	FY	727	0
X6	6.00p C	6.58p I	TW	104	FY	72S	0
X6	6.15p C	7.00p I	OZ	544	YQ	D9S	0
X6	6.49p C	7.52p I	FL	934	YQVM	CVR	0

FL 934 EFFECTIVE 1NOV

| X6 | 7.04p C | 8.07p I | FL | 934 | YQ | CVR | 0 |

FL 934 DISCONTINUED AFTER 31OCT

COMMUTER AIR CARRIERS

X67	7.00a K	8.05a I	ZV	812	Y	SWM	0
X67	9.30a C	11.10a I	XU	204	S	CNA	2
X67	10.45a K	1.15p S	EH	65	S	CNA	2
X67	12.35p C	2.10p I	ZV	815	Y	SWM	1
X67	2.20p K	3.25p I	ZV	833	Y	SWM	0
X67	5.00p K	6.20p S	EH	63	S	CNA	0
X67	5.45p C	7.20p I	XU	210	S	CNA	1
X67	6.45p K	7.55p I	ZV	803	Y	SWM	0

LAS VEGAS, NEV.   PST LAS

	8.25a	1.21p I	TW	274	FYK	72S	B	0
	10.05a	3.01p I	TW	414	FYK	72S	L	0
	1.25p	6.23p I	TW	558	YK	707	L	0
	2.20p	7.20p I	AA	206	FYD	727	L	0

LITTLE ROCK, ARK.   CST LIT

	8.15a	9.13a I	AA	232	FYK	72S	S/	0
	8.30a	9.26a I	DL	1664	FY	72S	S/	0
	12.55p	1.53p I	AA	464	FYD	727		0
	2.25p	3.22p I	DL	662	FY	72S		0
X6	4.00p	4.58p I	AA	422	FYD	72S		0
	6.28p	7.25p I	DL	438	FY	72S		0

LOS ANGELES, CALIF.   PST LAX

L LAX, B BUR, O ONT, S SMO, V VNY

	12.45a L	6.00a I	TW	72	FnYn	L10	S	0
	8.00a L	1.29p I	TW	136	FY	707	B	0
	8.25a L	1.54p I	AA	526	FYD	727	B	0
	9.10a L	3.36p I	TW	352	FY	72S	B	1
	10.10a L	3.37p I	TW	118	FY	707	L	0
	11.30a L	4.52p I	AA	390	FYD	727	L	0
	1.15p L	6.39p I	TW	100	FY	L10	L	0
	1.55p L	7.16p I	AA	256	FYD	727	L	0

LOUISVILLE, KY.   EST SDF

	8.10a	8.10a I	TW	541	FY	727	0
	11.10a	11.09a I	TW	571	FY	727	0
	11.35a	11.30a I	OZ	905	YQ	D9S	0
	4.50p	4.53p I	TW	269	FY	72S	0
X6	6.00p	6.05p I	AA	219	FYD	727	0
6	6.00p	6.05p I	AA	593	FYD	727	0
	10.12p	10.40p I	EA	647	FnYn	D9S	0

MADISON, WIS.   CST MSN

| X6 | 2.30p | 4.02p I | OZ | 511 | YQ | D9S | 1 |

MARION, ILL.   CST MWA

| X7 | 10.52a | 11.25a I | OZ | 958 | YQ | D9S | 0 |
| X6 | 8.22p | 9.42p I | OZ | 940 | YQ | D9S | 0 |

MEMPHIS, TENN.   CST MEM

X7	6.51a	7.45a I	DL	274	FnYn	72S	0
	8.43a	9.35a I	DL	1650	FY	D9S	0
	8.44a	9.35a I	RC	125	Y	DC9	0
	11.05a	11.57a I	RC	463	Y	DC9	0
	1.50p	2.42p I	DL	1606	FY	D9S	0
X6	3.05p	3.55p I	RC	218	Y	DC9	0
	4.41p	5.33p I	DL	814	FY	D9S	0
	5.35p	6.28p I	RC	243	Y	D9S	0
	8.11p	9.05p I	DL	308	FY	72S	0
X6	8.25p	9.15p I	RC	228	Yn	D9S	0

COMMUTER AIR CARRIERS

| X67 | 9.00a | 11.25a I | UX | 202 | Y | DHT | 1 |

MIAMI, FLA.   EST MIA

I MIA, P MPB

	6.23a I	9.42a I	EA	90	FY	727	B	2
	8.45a I	11.28a I	TW	485	FY	707	S	1
	1.32p I	3.55p I	OZ	548	YQ	D9S	S	1
	1.50p I	3.23p I	EA	690	FY	D9S	S	0
67	3.00p I	4.52p I	TW	497	Y	707	S	0
	3.52p I	5.44p I	TW	493	FY	727	D	0
	7.55p I	9.25p I	EA	92	FY	72S	S	0

MILWAUKEE, WIS.   CST MKE

X7	7.36a	8.40a I	OZ	901	YQ	D9S	S	0
	7.56a	9.00a I	RC	229	YQ	D9S	B	0
	12.00n	1.05p I	RC	192	Y	DC9	S	0
	12.25p	1.29p I	OZ	927	YQ	D9S	S	0
	5.05p	6.09p I	OZ	939	YQ	D9S	S	0
X6	6.10p	7.15p I	RC	225	YQ	DC9	S	0

MINNEAPOLIS/ST PAUL, MINN.   CST MSP

X7	7.05a	9.05a I	OZ	527	YQ	D9S	0
X7	7.15a	8.30a I	OZ	547	YQ	D9S	B	0
	7.25a	8.40a I	NW	460	Y	727	B	0
	11.20a	1.15p I	OZ	943	YQ	D9S	1
	11.35a	1.20p I	OZ	925	YQ	D9S	1
	3.30p	4.45p I	OZ	949	YQ	DC9	0
X6	5.30p	6.45p I	OZ	947	YQ	D9S	0
	5.35p	6.50p I	NW	466	Y	727	S	0
	6.20p	8.16p I	OZ	571	YQ	DC9	1
X6	7.30p	9.52p I	OZ	907	YQ	D9S	2

MOLINE, ILL.   CST MLI

| X7 | 6.45a | 7.34a I | OZ | 553 | YQ | D9S | 0 |
| X7 | 6.55a | 8.25a I | OZ | 559 | YQ | D9S | 1 |

CONT. NEXT COLUMN

From MOLINE, ILL.-CONT.   MLI

7	7.58a	8.40a I	OZ	595	YQ	D9S	0
	12.38p	1.20p I	OZ	925	YQ	D9S	0
X6	3.20p	4.02p I	OZ	511	YQ	D9S	0
X6	9.10p	9.52p I	OZ	907	YQ	D9S	0

COMMUTER AIR CARRIERS

| X67 | 10.45a | 11.45a I | UX | 402 | Y | HPJ | 0 |
| X6 | 6.25p | 7.25p I | UX | 112 | Y | HPJ | 0 |

NASHVILLE, TENN.   CST BNA

	10.15a	11.18a I	TW	453	FY	727	0
	11.53a	12.50p I	OZ	914	YQ	D9S	0
X6	4.00p	5.05p I	TW	557	FY	727	0

NEW ORLEANS, LA.   CST MSY

M MSY, N NEW

	7.10a M	9.35a I	DL	1650	FY	D9S	S	1
	12.30p M	2.05p I	OZ	504	YQ	D9S	L	0
	1.00p M	2.33p I	DL	426	FY	72S	L	0
	1.30p M	3.00p I	NW	467	Y	727	S	0
X6	6.20p M	7.50p I	OZ	503	YQ	D9S	D	0
	6.38p M	9.05p I	DL	308	FY	72S	S	1

NEW YORK N.Y/NEWARK, N.J.   EST NYC

J JFK, L LGA, E EWR

X7	7.00a I	8.38a I	TW	73	FY	72S	B	0
X7	7.40a I	10.21a I	AA	467	FYD	727	SB	1
	8.45a I	10.22a I	AA	239	FYD	727	B	0
X7	8.53a I	11.27a I	TW	119	FY	727	*	1

TW 119 * MEALS BS/S

	9.45a I	11.17a I	TW	155	FY	L10	S	0
	9.55a E	11.33a I	TW	205	FY	707	S	0
	12.00n I	1.33p I	AA	473	FYD	72S	L	0
	3.00p L	5.36p I	TW	233	FY	727	S	1
	3.30p L	6.09p I	AA	535	FYD	72S	S	1
	3.30p L	6.10p I	AA	243	FYD	72S	S	1
	3.50p L	5.27p I	TW	249	FY	707	S	0
X6	4.00p L	5.38p I	TW	477	FY	L10	S	0
6	4.00p L	5.43p I	TW	477	FY	72S	D	0
X6	5.05p L	6.48p I	AA	533	FYD	72S	D	0
X6	5.10p L	7.55p I	ML	97	FY	DC9	1

ML 87 EFFECTIVE 30OCT

X6	5.30p I	8.38p I	TW	365	FY	72S	D	1
	6.45p I	9.26p I	AA	251	FYD	72S	S	1
	7.25p I	9.07p I	TW	147	FY	72S	D	0
	9.10p I	10.47p I	TW	579	FnYn	72S		0

NORFOLK/VIRGINIA BEACH, VA.   EST ORF

| | 3.44p | 6.33p I | AL | 243 | Y | D9S | S | 2 |

OKLAHOMA CITY, OKLA.   CST OKC

R OKC, P PWA

| | 7.00a R | 9.10a I | TW | 436 | FY | 72S | B | 0 |

TW 436 DISCONTINUED AFTER 26OCT

| | 7.00a R | 9.11a I | TW | 436 | FY | 72S | B | 1 |

TW 436 EFFECTIVE 27OCT

	8.00a R	9.17a I	TW	140	FY	72S	B	S0
	12.13p R	1.30p I	TW	534	FY	72S	L	S0
	2.20p R	3.37p I	TW	358	FY	727	L	0
	4.35p R	6.43p I	TW	460	FY	72S		1

OMAHA, NEBR.   CST OMA

E OMA, M MIQ

	8.00a E	8.58a I	EA	273	FY	72S	S	0
X7	8.00a E	9.04a I	TW	410	FY	72S	B	S0
	12.17p E	1.15p I	EA	289	FY	727	0
X6	2.30p E	3.31p I	TW	370	FY	727	0
X6	5.43p E	7.52p I	FL	934	YQVM	CVR	1

FL 934 EFFECTIVE 1NOV

| | 5.50p E | 6.48p I | EA | 267 | FY | D9S | 0 |
| X6 | 5.58p E | 8.07p I | FL | 934 | YQ | CVR | 1 |

FL 934 DISCONTINUED AFTER 31OCT

COMMUTER AIR CARRIERS

| X67 | 11.35a E | 2.27p I | ZV | 815 | Y | SWM | 2 |

ORLANDO, FLA.   EST MCO

| | 7.31a | 9.42a I | EA | 90 | FY | 727 | B | 1 |
| | 10.20a | 1.33p I | EA | 774 | FY | 727 | L | 0 |

EA 774 EFFECTIVE 1NOV

	1.05p	2.15p I	OZ	918	YQ	D9S	L	0
	3.25p	5.43p I	TW	487	FY	72S	D	0
	6.00p	7.10p I	OZ	502	YQ	D9S	D	0

PADUCAH, KY.   CST PAH

COMMUTER AIR CARRIERS

X7	7.00a	8.05a I	UX	801	Y	DHT	0
	10.20a	11.25a I	UX	202	Y	DHT	0
6	12.50p	1.55p I	UX	313	Y	DHT	0
X67	1.30p	2.20p I	UX	707	Y	HS7	0
	1.30p	2.20p I	UX	727	Y	HPJ	0
	5.20p	6.25p I	UX	204	Y	DHT	0

PENSACOLA, FLA.   CST PNS

| | 11.30a | 3.04p I | EA | 200 | FY | 727 | 1 |

EA 200 DISCONTINUED AFTER 31OCT

| | 11.30a | 3.09p I | EA | 200 | FY | 72S | 1 |

EA 200 EFFECTIVE 1NOV

PEORIA, ILL.   CST PIA

7	7.30a	8.35a I	OZ	999	YQ	D9S	0
	7.50a	8.25a I	OZ	519	YQ	D9S	0
	9.30a	10.05a I	OZ	955	YQ	D9S	0
	12.08p	1.12p I	OZ	995	YQ	DC9	0
X6	12.08p	1.12p I	OZ	995	YQ	D9S	0
	5.35p	6.10p I	OZ	985	YQ	D9S	0

CONT. NEXT PAGE

TABLE 4-4

read one if need be.) Find out what scheduling possibilities you have and write them down. Go over to a phone, pull out your trusty roll, and call the airlines reservation lines directly. Make your reservation, find out the gate information, and you are once more off and running. (Note: Due to recent regulations, it may not always be possible in all situations to follow this procedure. When you or your travel agent makes the new reservation, you should be sure that the fares are the same, and that the new carrier will accept your old ticket coupon. If this is *not* the case, you will need to go to the main ticket counter of the new carrier in the terminal to have your ticket rewritten. Nonetheless, you'll still be far ahead of the crowd.)

Regular travelers save time by subscribing to the OAG *Pocket Flight Guide*, which lists the schedule for the top forty-eight U.S. cities (and top five Canadian cities) by traffic, and includes other cities by passenger volume. Tables 4-3 and 4-4 give sample pages. A one-year subscription currently costs $37 per year plus delivery and includes the monthly magazine, *Frequent Flyer*. For information write: Official Airlines Guide, 2000 Clearwater Dr., Oakbrook, IL 60521.

● *Make the Most Out of Getting Bumped*

If you are reserved on an overbooked flight, you risk being denied boarding despite your reservation. This is called "getting bumped." Your preflight call will protect you from this in most cases. But sometimes you will be delayed with a connecting flight or whatever and won't reach the gate in time.

○ *Make certain the airline tries to find you a seat*

Federal regulations now require the airline to ask for volunteers to take a later flight in return for money in an amount to be determined by the airlines at that time. The carrier is actually auctioning not taking the flight up to a maximum amount at its discretion. If someone doesn't mind delaying the trip and hears the right amount, you're in luck.

○ *Make certain you are reimbursed if you are bumped*

If you are still bumped, the airline MUST give you the flight to your next destination *plus* the full value of a one-way ticket (up to a maximum of $200). In addition, if the airline can't get you there within two hours of scheduled arrival (four hours for international travel), then compensation is doubled (to a maximum of $400).

Some business travelers use overbooking to make a little tax-free spending money. They purposely schedule popular flights with high probabilities of being overbooked. They arrive early to guarantee a seat. Then when the cash offers commence, they let the airline pay them to get off. One man told me he had been paid as much as $250 for his seat. Typically he receives between $50 and $150 EACH time he can schedule this type of flight. When he has some scheduling leeway, he can work this two or three times PER TRIP.

If you plan to do more traveling, you can use getting bumped to make even more money. The CAB now allows airlines to issue vouchers, passes, or travel certificates for more than the allowable maximums. The airlines love this because it costs them a relatively small amount of money with no cash outlay. And it benefits you because you can bargain the figure upward for a voucher. Getting an extra 50 percent with the voucher is not unusual.

● *Make the Airline Pay If You Are Bumped or Had a Flight Cancelled*

If you are bumped or stranded by a canceled flight, the airline should provide certain benefits. If you are delayed over a meal or overnight, the airline is obligated to feed and/or house you. Ask the ticket agent for meal vouchers or hotel accommodations. That's the key word, ASK.

● *Let the Airline Compensate for Misplaced Baggage*

If your bag isn't spit out the conveyor window before the belt stops, you have problems. You'll have to fill out tracer forms at the baggage desk. Normally your bag will be retrieved within twenty-four hours and almost always within two days. Don't offer to go back to the airport for the bag. Ask the airline to deliver it to your hotel or home to compensate you for the inconvenience. Also, if you're trapped away from home and need clothes, be it buying a dress or renting a tuxedo, let the airline know about it AND GIVE THEM A BILL. Airlines all have emergency money to disburse to passengers in distress.

● *Let the Airline Fetch Misplaced Articles*

If you leave something at the airport or in an airlines waiting area, go to that airline's main ticket counter for help. I left a coat on a chair in Las Vegas once and then flew to Palm Springs for a speech. When I went to the ticket counter, the airline called

Las Vegas free for me on their special phone line, had the people there look for the coat, and then had the coat put on the next flight over.

● **Have the Airline Help You Track Down Misplaced People**

Those special internal airlines phone lines can be of great help. If you miss a flight and someone is waiting to meet you, go to the ticket counter and ask them to have your party paged at your destination. You can tell your party the problem and save a long-distance phone call.

Most airline companies also have a special paging number you can call toll free. If you need to get a message to someone at an airport in another city, you can call the airline the person is using and have your party paged. Call the airline reservations number and ask for the toll-free paging number.

● **Get Wait-listed on the Earliest Flight Possible, as Soon as Possible**

You face other problems when trying to get on a full flight where none or little overbooking is allowed. For these full flights you may be put on a "wait list" to be given a reservation should someone else cancel beforehand or not show up at departure time. If you are flying in and out the same day and you want to get on a return flight that is full, get wait-listed for boarding when you arrive. Passengers are taken first come, first served, for a wait list. If you have your request time-stamped that morning, you stand an excellent chance of being first in line.

Also, get wait-listed on the *earliest flight* to your destination even if there is no chance you will get on the flight. The tendency is to wait-list for a later flight with fewer people on the list. What happens is that the people who missed the earlier flight are put at the top of the list for the next flight. So if you wait-list on the later flight, you will find yourself being shifted downward.

● *Talk to the "Passenger Service Representative"*

Flying can be a fast, convenient way to travel or it can be the world's most effective ulcer catalyst. If you have any problems, go over the gate or ticket agent's head. The Passenger Service Representative has more authority to solve your problem and can speed the solution.

● *Write the CAB*

Regardless of how you're treated, you have the option of sending complaint letters to the CAB's Bureau of Compliance and Consumer Protection, 1825 Connecticut Ave., Washington D.C. 20428. It can't adjudicate your problem, but your letter will be fed into the regular reports they provide the consumer, such as Table 4-2. In this way you will at least be helping future travelers.

■ AUTOMOBILE TRAVEL

America is still land of the free, home of the brave, and worshiper of the superhighway. The nation's roads carry 117 million autos, 31 million trucks, 5 million motorcycles, and 500,000 buses (most of which travel right in front of me). Despite government conservation programs, expanded train service, and some reduced airfares, nearly 87 percent of all intercity travel is done by car. And the bulk of commuters choose to turn the air brown spending as much as 10 percent of their waking hours driving themselves to work. So our love affair with rolling prerust continues.

■ BUYING A NEW CAR

At the time this is written, buying a new car cheaply is not too difficult. Dealers are finding it easier to sell a case of cholera than one of Detroit's finest. Still, should the buyer's market ever abate, you will once again need to know how to deal and wheel.

● *Find Out the Actual Dealer Cost*

The first item in your new car buying arsenal is the Automotive Invoice Service *New Car Cost Guide*. This monthly publication lists suggested retail prices, freight, and ACTUAL DEALER COST for every major car sold in America. All credit unions and banks have a copy. Dealers would gladly donate several superfluous organs to charity to get the AIS *Guide* off the streets. With it you no longer have to take the dealer's word about actual costs and profit margins.

If you can't find a copy of the AIS *Guide*, then obtain the *Consumer Reports* auto buying guide issue from the library or a friend. It lists the dealer cost as a percentage of the sticker price. You can take the sticker cost and perform multiplications on the auto and feature totals to obtain dealer cost. Add in the freight charge from the sticker and you are usually within $25 of dealer cost.

If you are too lazy to do either of these, insist on seeing the factory invoice for the car. Don't take a photocopy, note card, or whatever, no matter how official it looks. Most dealers list cost on internal documents at $200 to $300 over actual cost so they can show them to customers during the negotiations. Your "dealer cost" purchase may give several hundred dollars profit to the dealer. Without the dealer invoice, crank up Nelly Belle and roll on.

● *Select the Best Quality Manufacturer and Model*

Buying an auto without checking consumer publications is like getting married by mail. You deserve what you get. The best ratings source is the *Consumer Reports* buying guide issue.

● *Time Your Purchase*

In the golden days when the U.S. auto industry was not rushing to catch up with foreign competitors, the best time to buy a new car was at the end of the model year during close-out sales. With the rapid inflation during recent years, this is no longer valid. Factories pass along price increases as many as four or five times during model years. Cars delivered in September can be $500 or $600 cheaper than a car shipped in June. Fall is now the best time of year to buy a new car.

Also, time your negotiations and purchase to occur late in the month. Although salespeople have a wide range of incentives which vary from dealer to dealer, manufacturer to manufacturer, most have some type of bonus plan tallied on a monthly basis. The salesperson is more likely to bargain away part of the commission if he or she is close to a performance bonus number.

● *Get Control of the Sale*

With dealerships all over the country taking the deep six, you are in a great position to bargain. When you walk into the sales office, you know the exact dealer cost. Don't just start bargaining, make the salesperson sit five minutes or so while you pretend to do some figuring with a calculator and pad of paper. Finally, write a few digits, circle them and announce, "Now I know your exact cost. How much do you want for the car?"

If the salesman tells you to make an offer, respond, "Wait a minute. You're selling the car, I'm not. I don't price your goods—you should. Now in this market I'd like to pay dealer cost and let you make your cut off warranty repairs and factory bonuses. Now if you don't sell it to me for that, then you better give me a price."

If the salesperson disputes your dealer cost figure, offer to call the bank or credit union and double-check your price with the AIS *Guide*. It stops that nonsense immediately. There is obviously much more to bargaining, but with this you are in control of the sale and have the dealer relationship off on the right footing.

■ BUYING A USED CAR

A friend of mine lists selling used cars as one of the three lowest forms of human endeavor. While there are reputable dealers and individuals selling used cars, more room for abuse exists in this industry than

in most any other. Anyone buying a used car
without a test drive and mechanic's diagnostic check
should be given milk and cookies and be led off
before getting hurt. If you're trading with a dealer,
the Better Business Bureau can help. But where the
real bargains lie is in buying from individuals.

● *Know the Used Car's Value*

The used car equivalent to the AIS *Guide* is the
National Automobile Dealers Association *Used Car
Guide*, frequently called the "blackbook." It lists the
average trade-in, average loan value, and retail price
for all makes of cars. Prices are updated every two
weeks, so it is easy to get a recently outdated copy
from your banker. The condition of a used car will
cause its value to vary up or down from the
blackbook price, but you will have a working point
to begin bargaining.

● *Buy from Desperate or Discouraged Sellers*

Chuck, a reformed greaser and the world's greatest
used car buyer, suggests never falling in love with
any car. You must be flexible enough to find the
right seller—desperate or discouraged—and get your
deal. His rule is: *Never answer a newspaper ad until it is
two weeks old, or until it has appeared for the third week
in a row.*

Reasonably priced cars are quickly bid up and
bought up. If you call and the car is gone, you didn't
want it anyway. What you will find with Chuck's
rule are cars with flaws or cars with unreasonable
asking prices. After several demoralizing weeks of
nonselling, you can frequently buy a car for less than
earlier bids which were rejected.

● *Play Poor but Bring Cash*

Always wear old clothes to look at a used car. Cough and wheeze. You want to look like a vagrant. When the owner quotes the asking price, whistle in astonishment and shake your head. Don't say anything, let the owner react. Always bring cash, preferably in small, crumpled bills. Chuck uses a ragged shoe box to hold his money. The nice thing about cash is that a "take it or leave it" cash offer of $1,000 is often equal to an "I promise to bring the money Monday" offer of $1,200.

■ KEEPING YOUR CAR RUNNING

When and what you have to do to keep your car running is carefully spelled out in the owner's manual. How you get it done is another matter. Unfortunately, the auto requires nurturing and occasional first aid which can eat up your time and money.

● *Fill Up After a Tanker Delivery*

Never fill up when a tanker truck is going to make a delivery. With gas supplies tight, stations are pumping out of the bottom of their storage tanks for the first time in years. At month end or right before a tanker delivery you may be getting high octane sludge and dirt which will gum up your car. A single bad tank of gas can ruin an entire trip. Find out when your favorite station gets deliveries and fill up afterward.

● *Make the Inspector Want to Pass Your Car*

In states requiring an inspection by an approved mechanic, you can minimize the chances of being rejected on a technicality by proper planning. Take your car in fifteen to twenty minutes before closing when the service bays are empty and being cleaned out. An inspection doesn't get anything dirty and the mechanic will want to finish quickly. If this doesn't work out for you, pick a place with busy pumps. After five to ten interruptions, the mechanic will slam the car through just to be rid of it.

● *Get Your Car Worked On First*

It's best to use a mechanic who schedules appointments and then keeps his schedule. There are as many of these as there are left-handed neurosurgeons who skateboard. If you are dealing with the rest of the shops, set up a morning appointment and let the mechanic know you are bringing the car in the night before. Park the car *in front of an empty bay*. The next morning the mechanic has the choice of moving yours to get to another car or pulling your car right in. You've made it easier for him to work on yours first.

Drop the keys into the mail slot in an envelope with written instructions of what is to be done. At the bottom of the note remind the mechanic that no additional work or work over a certain amount is authorized without a phone call. Also tell the mechanic that you will wish to inspect any old parts. This makes you sound more knowledgeable.

Finally, keep a carbon of your note. If you come to get your car and find an exorbitant bill, refuse to pay on the grounds that the work was unauthorized. Show them the note if there is an argument. If they say they didn't read the note, remind them they had to read your note in order to know what to do. If they claim to have lost your note, show them your carbon.

● *Avoid the License Bureau Crowd*

The world is full of procrastinators who drive cars. A license bureau clerk said half the business occurs in the five-day period covering the last three and first two days of each month. Monday and Friday are also busy days as many people take off to enjoy a three-day weekend. During any one day, lunchtime is busiest. To avoid the crowd, visit the license bureau in the middles—middle of the month, midweek, in midmorning or midafternoon.

■ **KEEPING YOUR CAR MOVING**

The "mobile" part of the word automobile is sometimes a cruel lie. Anyone who has sucked fumes for several hours during rush hour realizes that the car is often the auto-immobile. If you hit the rat race A.M. and P.M., you are probably tired of being a rat. You will also have practiced some of these tips as a matter of natural selection:

● *Minimize Stop and Go Intersections*

According to the AAA, every stop sign on your daily route (either way) costs you $31 per year in extra gasoline spent slowing down and speeding up. If you have to inch forward in a long line of cars, the cost is even greater depending upon how long the line. In addition, each stop sign eats up about twenty-five of your precious seconds. Stoplights take even more time. The typical large city stoplight cycle is eighty-five seconds during normal traffic hours and sixty seconds during rush hour. Each traffic light you eliminate from your route can save a minute a day, or four or more hours per year.

● *Analyze Flow Patterns*

Highway traffic tends to move faster on the outside lanes before the interchanges and faster on the inside lanes afterward. With a little judicious (and careful) lane changing, you can always be in the faster moving lane. New York cabbies seem to have an extra twist on their DNA chain which allows them to pick the best highway or city lane no matter what the situation.

● *Pick the More Level Route*

Traffic engineers know that hilly terrain causes the "accordion effect." Cars slow going uphill and speed downhill. Because of the delay in speeding back up due to human reaction times, a slowdown develops. Send the lead car in a line of 300 during rush hour over a series of hills varying from 40 to 55 mph and the 300th car will be crawling along stop and go at 5 mph.

● *Adjust Your Travel Time*

In most cities there is a rush hour, an early rush hour to beat the rush hour, and the late rush hour to avoid the early and main rush hour. One cummuter who lives in Princeton Junction, New Jersey, and works in White Plains, New York, told me a one-half-hour difference in departure time saves him fifty minutes in travel time to or from work. Try shifting your departure time up or back to see if you can reduce trip time.

● *Scare Off Tailgaters*

One of the great hazards in traffic is the tailgater who needs to be close enough to your back bumper to inspect it for rust spots. To get this driver off your tail try turning on your emergency flashers. This often makes him wake up and back off. If that doesn't work and it is daytime, turn on your headlights. From the rear this appears as if you've hit the brakes.

■ KEEPING YOUR CAR PARKED

Parking lots are so gracious and bighearted. You pay them to watch your car but they aren't responsible if anything bad happens to it. Since you are still responsible for your car, here are a few parking tips.

● *Make Your Car Unstartable*

You can't keep a thief out of your car. So the best technique is to make your car appear unstartable. Have your mechanic install a switch which connects to your starter (not your fuel or ignition or you'll have problems if it trips accidentally while you're moving). Hide the switch under the dash or disguise it as a radio or light button. When the starter won't engage, the thief will think your battery is dead and move on to better game.

● *Leave Only an Ignition Key*

When leaving your auto with a carhop, give only the ignition key. Your trunk key can be used to swipe your spare and emergency kit. If your house keys are on the ring, copies can be made and your address obtained from information in the car.

● *Say You'll Only Be Gone a Minute*

Attendants have been known to replace a new car's equipment with old parts if they know they have time.

● *Write Down the Car's Mileage Openly in Front of the Attendant*

Write your mileage down on the parking ticket before you give your key to the attendant. He will see this and think twice about taking your car on a joy ride. Attendants have been known to borrow cars for use during robberies or to rent out rides in sports cars or luxury cars to friends. If the attendant sees you write down the mileage and thinks you'll be back shortly, he will be hesitant to risk playing with your car.

■ THE TICKET GAME

Sometimes the only way to get from here to there faster is to waste our nation's precious resources in an un-American manner by speeding. This means you are now a participant with your law enforcement professionals in the time-honored ticket game. There are a number of ways to avoid getting ticketed while pushing the speedometer upward from 55.

● *Don't Speed Through Potential Traps*

Certain locations make ideal speed traps, so you will see officers there periodically year after year. Typically they are near a police station, provide a good view of the road, have a place to hide, and have a convenient turn-around area for the officer to come back and set up again.

There are also places which officers call "cherry patches." A cherry patch is a location where the average driver will violate the law. For example, there may be an obscured speed limit sign, a sharp reduction in speed on a highway going into town, a confusing *No Left Turn* sign or whatever. My police officer evening college students all had a favorite location (which they "hoarded" from their friends) where they could pick up some easy tickets if they were running behind their "unofficial quotas."

● *Be Careful of* When *You Speed*

In *The Ticket Book* former police officer Rod Dornsife estimates that 85 percent of all tickets are written in the first two to four hours of the police shift. Officers want to get their ticketing out of the way so they can relax later on and only answer emergency calls or catch up on paperwork.

● *Don't Stand Out in a Crowd*

Fast-looking cars such as Porsches, Corvettes, 280Z's or jacked-up hot rods are more likely to be stopped than an LTD station wagon. Police also tend to pick off the leader or trailer in a long line of fast-moving cars. It's too much trouble to blast into the middle of the group to get someone.

● *Don't Get Greedy*

Typically, you can go 5 to 10 mph over the speed limit without too much risk of a ticket. The police would rather grab folks really stomping on the pedal.

Tickets written for just over the 55 mph limit are often thrown out anyway because ordinary car speedometers are not that accurate. In fact, speedometers tend to underestimate miles per hour at highway speeds and overestimate at lower city speeds.

● Get a CB

Depending upon how well you like the chatter, you can get a CB radio (or just a receiver and maintain some level of personal dignity) and let the other drivers tattle on the police for you.

● Get Out of the Ticket

All is not lost once the police officer gets out of the patrol car and strolls up to your window. It's just that now you're on the defense instead of the offense.

○ Be polite

Don't scream, "Why aren't you out catching muggers and rapists instead of trapping law-abiding citizens accidentally going 8 mph over the speed limit?" Be polite and hope the officer is riding high on his monthly quota and will only give you a warning. Try an excuse, but don't expect it to bring tears to anyone's eyes. Police officers write between 50,000 and 100,000 tickets in a career and have heard it all.

○ Pinch the baby

A quick-thinking wife saved a ticket with this trick. Faced with a screaming child, the officer closed the ticket book and took off without a word. Another woman told me how her youngest child got hysterical when the woman was stopped for a ticket. As the officer approached, the little girl started yelling, "Oh, don't shoot my Mommy! Mommy, Mommy, is he going to kill you? Get away, get away. EEEEEEEEEEEK!" The officer stared in disbelief and then stomped off with a disgusted look.

○ *Hope for a technicality*

Once the officer starts writing, save your breath. Tickets are numbered and must be accounted for (to discourage ticket fixing). If you are ticketed, write down the officer's name and pertinent details. They may be useful should you decide to contest the ticket—something well worth your while. A single ticket can nearly double the insurance rates of a driver in the lowest risk bracket. Approximately one in 100 tickets go to trial, and of these, about 30 percent of the drivers win. If your ticket is based on radar alone, you have a one in four chance of winning on some technicality.

○ *Contest the ticket*

If you decide to contest a ticket, be prepared to state your case clearly and with as many facts as possible. An industrial engineer was ticketed for speeding by a police officer using painted road marks and a stopwatch to determine speed. The engineer brought in a diagram of the road showing how bad the officer's viewing angle was and what the inaccuracies could be from that angle. He then had both the judge and the officer time a light bulb that was controlled by an electronic timer system the engineer had borrowed from work. Both the judge and officer failed to get the same result twice. The engineer then suggested that the officer's view was poor, and that he could have mistimed the interval. The engineer won his case by *creating doubt*, which is all that needs to be done.

You might not be able to present a case this well yourself, but perhaps the officer won't show and you can ask for a dismissal of the case. When in doubt, if insurance premiums or important driver's license points are at stake, get a lawyer near the courthouse who specializes in traffic cases to handle your trial.

■ AUTOMOBILE INSURANCE

Buying any kind of insurance is aggravating because comparison shopping is so difficult. Every time you go for a bid you have asked another agent to come pounding down on you with his full line of services.

● *Comparison Shop*

The easiest way to comparison shop is to check with the State Board of Insurance. Each state monitors or regulates insurance companies for price and service. The state agency will be happy to pass on cost figures and complaint statistics, and frequently will provide regular publications containing this information which you can request on a regular basis. After studying this information, you can then call the one or two companies that seem to fit your needs best.

● *Find Out the Threshold Amount*

An item you need to know in dealing with an insurance company is its "threshold" procedures for claims. If your claim exceeds the threshold in any one period, your next year's premiums are raised or your policy might not be renewed. For example, if you had $550 in damages with a deductible of $200, your claim would be $350. If the threshold amount was $300, you might save several hundred dollars by estimating damages at only $499 and filing a claim under the $300 threshold. Some companies use their own damage estimators and won't let you do this. So find out what the threshold rules are for your current company or for any company you're considering switching to.

■ DRIVING LESSONS

The previous section on automobile travel may not have applied to you. Incredible as it might seem with millions of cars on the roads, there is a large number of people in the U.S. who cannot drive. The driving lesson industry sees a steady flow of adults who decide to finally take the plunge and climb behind the wheel.

The busiest times of the year for scheduling lessons are May and June. The nondriver sees summer coming and realizes that he or she will be stranded. The best time for taking lessons is in the late fall when the training people aren't busy and the weather hasn't gotten too severe. The student can then sign up for later lessons during poor winter driving conditions—when a few lessons are given—to learn the specialized driving techniques required in their area.

If you decide to call for lessons, avoid Mondays. People don't drive because of fear. Driving school instructors tell me that Mondays are their busiest phone days because the nondriver has spent all weekend getting encouragement from the family and getting up the courage to call.

■ TRAIN TRAVEL

Never take the train!

"When the Nixon people said it's about time we started running the post office like a business, I didn't know they meant Lockheed and Chrysler!"

–Joe King

5

Service with a Smile

I've always appreciated the late J. C. Penney's concept of good service as expressed to his store managers, "Either you or your replacement will greet the customer within the first sixty seconds." In an increasingly specialized world we are more and more dependent upon others for helping us get things done. Some businesses, such as restaurants, offer us something we can get more cheaply at home but are willing to pay extra for because of the service. Others, such as the post office, have a near monopoly and charge whatever their inefficiency drives the price to.

Getting the extra service we are paying for or getting the minimum service we *must* pay for is no easy matter. Service people act as if they're doing US the favor by agreeing to work on our appliance. The restaurant host or hostess condescends to give us a table only a spilled tray away from the kitchen and dirty dishes bucket. Lawyers will call us back if we're persistent. In all we get pushed around because we are unable to become obnoxious enough to get the attention we feel we deserve. Fortunately, there are other ways.

■ FINANCIAL SERVICES

Competition for our deposit dollar is fierce and getting stronger all the time. The lobbies of many thrift institutions have so many gifts and premiums it would make a TV game show producer proud. The government has loosened up a bit on what alternatives thrift institutions may offer to customers and the marketing department has taken it from there.

● *Shop for a Thrift Institution*

Every institution seems to offer the same services. Yet the actual cost to you can vary greatly. With the recent approval of NOW accounts (Negotiated Order of Withdrawal), thrift institutions are battling for consumer deposits formerly kept in checking accounts not paying interest. But they price these and other services with a bewildering array of hidden or unexplained costs and procedures. Find out the following:

1. How is interest calculated? The maximum bank interest, for example, is currently 5¼ percent. But this doesn't mean 5¼ percent is all you will earn. Interest can be calculated on a 360-day year or a 365-day year, which is better. Some ads state interest is paid daily, but *compounded* quarterly. Compounding daily is best. Ask your bank, savings and loan, or credit union for its *annual percentage yield*. This will give you a number you can compare from place to place.

2. What amount is interest calculated on? The majority of institutions pay on average daily balance. But some pay on the lowest balance over a period of time which is usually lower than your average daily balance.

3. What is the minimum deposit? With NOW or checking accounts, some institutions require a minimum balance either in the account or in another savings account. With the higher market rates available in other savings instruments, your bank deposit costs you money. The lower this minimum deposit requirement, generally the better.

4. How is the minimum deposit calculated? Some institutions figure the minimum deposit amount as an average balance over a certain period. Your account could be empty for a time as long as it was correspondingly higher than the minimum for an equal amount of time. Other institutions figure the minimum as a floor figure, charging you fees if you fall below the minimum even once. The average method is much more flexible.

5. What are costs for related services? In comparing services, ask about the cost of related fees, such as penalties for going under the minimum, cost of checks, flat monthly service charges, stopping payment on a check, funds transfers, wiring funds, or paying an overdrawn check. Find out the fees *before* you open an account. Also, ask about extra services such as postage-paid bank by mail envelopes. Some institutions still provide these.

● *Bank by Mail or Drop Box*

There is no reason to ever set foot in a lobby with a deposit. For 18 cents you can mail everything and have the receipt mailed back. All you need do is endorse the check, write "for deposit only at," and add the institution name. You can hardly start your car for 18 cents so you save both time and money.

The drop box is your next best alternative for deposits. Every institution has a slot for night deposits after office hours. Just be careful if anyone nearby seems to be loitering. The night depository area is perfect for thieves waiting for business people making deposits of evening receipts.

● *Use the "Ugly Teller"*

Depending upon the state you live in, you may have access to institutions with automated teller terminals. The two types are stand-alone or on-line to the computer. The stand-alone unit allows you to withdraw a limited amount of money and make deposits which are handled the next morning, and the automated unit allows you to withdraw to a limit (usually higher than stand-alone units) based upon your account balance stored in the computer.

I refuse to wait in banking lines. I haven't set foot in my S & L during banking hours in the four years since they installed an ugly teller. My deposits are made by mail and withdrawals are made evenings or weekends from the machine. I use the outside machine even during banking hours. It's amazing to see people stacked up inside and the machine outside ready for use. The human body did not evolve for millions of years just to stand in a bank line or to sit in a row of cars waiting to make a deposit.

● *Avoid Busy Times*

If you *must* go in a thrift institution to transact business other than routine deposits or withdrawals, pick the slack time periods. Mondays and Fridays are the busiest times of the week, with noontime presenting each day's biggest crush of people. The last day before a holiday is also overcrowded as people prepare for their days off. On a monthly basis, the first three days of each month and the 15th are busy days. This is because pension and government checks are issued the 1st of the month and the 1st and 15th see so many paychecks and loan payments submitted. In general, avoid these times.

■ **GETTING A LOAN**

Although you should "never borrow money needlessly," you can always get a little help from a friend. Ignoring a mortgage, all of us at one time or another have fallen short of cash and have needed a loan. The whole loan application process is somewhat of a mystery to us. We submit the forms, then wait for several weeks until we get an answer. Typically the only explanation for a refusal is a preprinted form with one of twenty or so boxes checked.

Banker Joseph Smith, author of *How to Borrow Money from a Bank,* feels that most people don't know how to deal with a loan officer. If you understand how the loan officer thinks, he told me in an interview, you can greatly increase your chances of getting a loan. For example, everything revolves around what Smith calls the credit triangle:

1. Capacity. Is your financial situation such that you will be able to repay the loan? Will this loan overextend your finances?

2. Collateral. What is the worth of what you are offering to guarantee the loan? The lending institution isn't in business to repossess used property, but should you default, what is the institution's financial risk?

3. Character. Are you honest? Have you been truthful? Are you not only able to repay, but are you *willing* to repay should there be problems?

● **Get Personal**

What Smith suggests is developing a good long-term working relationship with the loan officer of your savings institution. Get to know him or her like you would your minister or doctor. Don't talk to the loan officer only when you are in need, stop by to chat briefly whenever you are in the office. Update the loan officer on your financial status and let this important person get to know you. You will have established number 3 in the credit triangle ahead of time.

The loan officer knows that people aren't always honest about their financial situation. Don't make the mistake of coming in without all the proper information or of trying to deceive the loan officer. Lay it all out in the open and see if this person with whom you've developed a good relationship can help you. All decisions are made based on these questions, "What will be this person's reaction in the worst possible case? Will I get paid?" Help the loan officer make this character judgment.

● *Avoid Getting Turned Down*

Regulation B of the Equal Credit Opportunity Act specifies what reasons are valid for refusing a loan application and also specifies outlines on how these must be presented to you. Normally all you will receive is a checklist of the twenty items with the appropriate one marked. Some of them are clear, but others require an explanation. I interviewed several loan officers to get their interpretation of each rejection reason so that you might make yourself more creditworthy:

1. Credit application incomplete. Don't appear slipshod by sending the application in incomplete. This is like noticing the pilot of your airliner has his fly open.
2. Insufficient credit references. You may not have a credit rating. The fastest and cheapest way to establish one is to apply for a 90-day note secured against your deposits (the institution can't lose) in the amount of several thousand dollars. Pay it off on time and you will have a good start.
3. Unable to verify credit references. If you include a personal loan from an individual in your credit references, make certain that person can be contacted by the institution. Give a phone number or address along with the name. If you don't know how to contact the individual anymore, don't list that person.
4. Temporary or irregular employment. Changing jobs regularly in upward moves isn't a

problem. But not having a predictable income alerts the loan officer to potential problems.

5. Unable to verify employment. When applying, give the name and phone number of the person verifying your job. Warn that person ahead of time that a call will be coming so that you don't accidentally surprise the person and get the wrong reference.

6. Length of employment. This is a factor only when you don't have a continuous job history from the time you left school. If there have been several periods of unemployment, then time on the job will be a factor.

7. Insufficient income. A general guideline is that no person should have more than 35 percent of gross monthly salary tied up in fixed payments (including home mortgage). If the loan will put you over that percent, you will likely be refused.

8. Excessive obligation. Another measure of financial capacity is that you shouldn't have more than half of your gross annual salary tied up in consumer debts (excluding home mortgage).

9. Unable to verify income. This occurs only when you are unable to verify your income satisfactorily through your employer or from self-employed accounting records.

10. Inadequate collateral. The collateral you propose may not be valuable enough to secure the loan or may not be liquid enough to turn quickly into cash should you default.

11. Too short a period of residence. This reason isn't used too often anymore. Our mobile society has lessened the importance of predicting loan repayment from maintaining one residence.

12. Temporary residence. The institution doesn't want to loan money to someone and not be able to track the borrower down later if there is a default.

13. Unable to verify residence. A letter with your name on it will suffice.

14. No credit file. See number 2.

15. Insufficient credit file. See number 2.

16. Delinquent credit obligations. If you are already delinquent in repaying some type of debt, no loan officer will touch you. If you need a consolidation loan to meet your debts, apply for it BEFORE you default on one.

17. Garnishment, attachment, foreclosure, repossession, or suit. The first four are the loan world's kiss of death. An active suit may be a factor depending upon its nature. If you have a small business and face a nuisance suit, the loan officer may ignore it. But if you have a possibility of being hit with a heavy judgment which could wipe you out, the loan officer will not take the chance.

18. Bankruptcy. Greater numbers of people in financial difficulties are choosing bankruptcy as a way to obtain a new start. The new bankruptcy law is more liberal concerning what you may keep and makes bankruptcy appear more attractive. If you declare bankruptcy, don't plan on getting a straight loan EVER again.

The loan companies (at higher interest rates) will be your only alternative.

19. We do not grant credit to any applicant on the terms and conditions you request. The institution doesn't have to make a special deal for you. As long as *nobody* gets a loan on your terms, there is no discrimination.

20. Other. Should you not have one of the above items checked on the refusal form, the loan institution must specify why you have been denied the loan.

In addition to the information listed above, you have the right to find out what outside sources of credit information were used to evaluate your application. You also have the right to make a written request within sixty days of receipt of the notice of refusal, asking for the adverse information used to reject your application. This is what the law requires.

The lending institution may have a procedure for evaluating your application that isn't reflected in the checklist above. Loan companies, for example, want their office managers not to use judgment only. They use a "credit scoring system" which assigns point values to various factors and then makes a go/no-go decision based upon the total points. The exact number of points varies from company to company, but Table 5-1 illustrates the scoring approach used by one company.

Examining this credit scoring system allows you to draw some important conclusions. First, poor trade rating hurts you more than a good trade rating helps you. Throughout the table, having positive credit history factors is never as important as having no credit history problems. Second, the commonly used

Factor	Amount	Value
1. Number of favorable credit references	0	0
	1	+1
	2 or more	+2
2. Number of recent credit inquiries	0	+4
	1-2	0
	3-5	–1
	6 or more	–4
3. Number of good trade ratings	0	-1
	1	0
	2 or more	+1
4. Number of poor trade ratings	0	0
	1	–4
	2 or more	–7
5. Number of past-due balances	0	0
	1 or more	–3
6. Age of oldest credit-rated account	0 to 6 mos.	0
	7 mos. to 2 yrs.	+1
	2 yrs. to 6 yrs.	+2
	6 yrs. or more	+4
7. Housing Status	Rent	0
	Own	+2
8. Time on job	0 to 18 mos.	0
	18 to 84	+1
	85 or more	+2
9. Total annual income	Under 12,000	0
	12,001 to 19,000	+1
	19,001 or more	+2
10. Banking relationship	no checking	–2
	no savings	0
	checking & savings	+3
11. Number of poor credit references	0	0
	1	–2
	2 or more	–4

Table 5-1

factors such as home owning (number 7) and time on the job (number 8) are relatively unimportant. Third, sheer number in credit ratings doesn't help much. You are better off to have one good trade account for six or more years (number 6) than to have five good trade ratings (number 3).

Finally, you can harm yourself by innocently applying for retail credit or for a loan at several places at once. If you have a high number of recent inquiries you might appear to be getting turned down for a loan at place after place. Or it may seem as if you might get overextended with credit if all your inquiries are from trade accounts.

So consider how your actions affect the credit triangle. Make certain you have a checking and savings account with good ratings (number 10). Keep your credit applications well-spaced so that you don't have a flurry of inquiries at the credit bureau. Maintain your longest held credit account paid up on time and think carefully before canceling it. Most importantly, take care of your financial needs BEFORE problems begin showing up on your record. You may be in need of money but have already worked your way out of any chance to get some.

■ RESTAURANT SERVICE

Poor service at a restaurant is particularly galling since you can have bad service (or no service) at home for free. Yet, dining out is one of the important social customs we enjoy and anticipate.

● *Getting a Reservation*

If a restaurant is very popular or if you plan to visit it on a weekend evening, you may have trouble getting reservations. The maître d' has seen it all, every trick, every intimidation ploy, every possible way to get into a full restaurant. Still, insiders know a few alternatives that work:

○ *Flattery may get you everywhere*

If you are from out of town (or even if you're not), call up the maître d' and ask for a reservation. If he has no openings, tell him that you are from out of town and won't be able to visit the restaurant at a later date. Tell him your friends recommend it most highly and that you would love to dine there if at all possible—you had been looking forward to it. If the chef has a specialty, mention that you had been hoping to try it. What you are betting on is that pride will take over. When so many Americans dull their taste buds with cocktails and then wolf the food anyway, a competent host is thrilled to see an interested diner.

○ *Ask for your usual table*

Call and apologize for not having been there for so long. Ask for your usual table at the convenient time. Tell the maître d' you know you're calling late but he's always been able to take care of you in the past. Offer to shift your arrival up or back slightly if it will help. Maybe the host will think he's forgotten you and will work you in. If so, remember him with a gratuity and it may work again.

○ *Have someone with an accent call*

It sounds ridiculous, but it works! Have someone with an accent, or someone who can effectively fake one, call up for reservations. "Signore Salami would like to dine at Le Château Blanc tonight at eight. Will you have a suitable table ready?" "Signore Salami" plays a lot better than Bob and Sue Belle Salami. To the host, the *signore* sounds like he might be someone important and add a little class to the joint.

● *Beat the Crowd*

Face it, if you insist on going to a popular dining spot Friday or Saturday evening, it better have a good bar because you're going to wait. The slowest times of the week are Sunday noon or Monday noon and evening. Monday evenings are particularly slow during football season due to the weekly ABC game. Seasonally, the slowest months for the restaurant business are January and June through September. People are too broke after Christmas and have been overeating anyway. And the summer months see people out enjoying the weather or barbecuing their hearts out.

A good time to walk right in to a first-class restaurant is the night of a moderate to heavy snowfall. Bad weather always knocks out the restaurant trade. Unlike an entertainment feature, patrons can always come another night.

● *Minimize Your Wait*

We've all waited in the bar of some ritzy restaurant slopping down cocktails only to be blitzed by the time we're seated. Often you can't avoid waiting, but you can shorten the interval until being seated.

○ *Examine the waiting list*

The typical host or hostess gives out waiting estimates like politicans give out promises—indiscriminately and with no thought of having to answer for them. I've seen the number of people waiting for a table double and heard the hostess drone on, "Twenty minutes . . . twenty minutes . . . twenty minutes . . ." Forget the time estimate. Check out the waiting crowd, then look over the size of the place. If you are a party of four or less, the name list alone will help you estimate the wait. If there is an odd or large number of you, ask how many parties your size are ahead of you and then also how many tables they have which can seat a party your size. You might get a dirty look for the interrogation, but you can make your go/no-go decision logically.

○ *Call ahead with a special order*

Another way to insure you will not be kept waiting past your reservation is to call in a special food order earlier in the day. Most fine restaurants allow regular clients to order special dishes off the menu which take a longer time than normal to prepare. The chef starts your meal in anticipation of your arrival so it will be ready on time. When you check in, remind the maître d' that you have a special dish in preparation and will need to be seated promptly. This will always work!

○ *Give yourself a title*

Titles may or may not pull much weight with the host. I have talked to all types of people with titles such as Dr., Judge, Gen., Col., and Rev. and asked if their title helped them. Strangely enough, and for no explicable reason, Judge seems to work the best. Academia, medicine, the military, and religion don't carry as much impress value as the legal system. So if you feel sporting, list yourself as "Judge Salami." For all anyone knows, you judge dog shows or Hot Wheels races and are overly pretentious. All you're doing is getting in on the "Kentucky Colonel" action.

○ *Come in right before the next wave*

Patrons seem to arrive at restaurants in waves, depending upon the nearby entertainment. For one of your regular spots, you will begin to see the ebb and flow arrival pattern. For example, a restaurant near a theater has a large early dinner crowd and will suddenly thin out right before 8:00 P.M. Arriving at 7:30 or scheduling reservations for 7:45 should result in no more than a small wait.

● *Be Creative in Getting Faster Service*

Your waiter or waitress is often at the mercy of a manager caught shorthanded by unreliable help. You can sit in the middle of a restaurant as invisible as a ghost in a snowstorm trying to get the attention of a suddenly snow-blind waiter scurrying by. Here are a few ideas for breaking out of the drift:

○ *Tell the waiter you're in a hurry*

When you have the waiter's attention during ordering, tell him you are in a hurry and will appreciate anything he can do to expedite your order. After your order is completed, remind the waiter once again of your special needs.

○ *Treat the waiter/waitress as a person*

Most of us treat waiters and waitresses as non-people. After they introduce themselves we can't remember the name. After they walk off we don't know what they looked like. "Excuse me, sir. Could you send our waiter over?"

"I AM your waiter."

"Ah, yes . . ."

Treat the waiter or waitress as you would someone you met at a party. Call them by name and even introduce yourselves back. You will be amazed at the service you receive.

○ *Call the manager over*

If you are being ignored, there is no reason to keep begging your waiter for service or to stiff him on the tip later when your meal is ruined. Ask for the manager or get up and find him to explain your problem. Remain calm and orderly while stating that you thought he would not condone such service and knew he would want to hear about what was happening.

○ *Ask for a black tablecloth*

If the manager comes over, request a black tablecloth. Of course he'll ask why and you can respond, "In memory of our waiter who must have died." If this is delivered with decent humor everyone will get a chuckle and the manager can get the message back to the waiter.

○ *Use the truck driver plan*

Two over-the-road truckers told me how they solved their slow restaurant service problem. Time out of the cab is money to them, plus they eat out too much to enjoy it. So they developed this little scam to insure prompt service:

One of them sits down and looks mean while the other gets a waitress to one side. He then goes into his spiel: "Look, I don't want to alarm you or anything, but this has really been a problem. My partner has this thing about slow service. He just goes nuts when he has to wait for his food. He dumps plates upside down, throws food all over, breaks up chairs and stuff. You can't imagine what it's like. I'm stuck traveling with him and I can't do anything about it. Could you make sure we get our food pretty quick? I'm sick and tired of this and it would sure save a lot of problems." The trucker tells me the service they see is spectacular.

○ *Stand up at the table*

This works for just about any situation, whether problems at the table, no food, or no bill. At a crowded New Year's Eve dinner my party was seated at a wobbly table which swayed almost a foot back and forth. We kept asking someone to move us but with no results. So we all stood up at the table to the distraction of the other guests. The manager finally came over and we showed him the table. We were immediately seated elsewhere. To our amusement, another party sat down, discovered the wobbly table with some dismay, then endured it wordlessly rather than make a scene.

○ *Don't special-order "fast" foods*

A cook at one of the hamburger emporiums explained that she and her cronies hated special orders.

In back, everyone has a specific duty station in the assembly process, i.e., someone who heats the buns, a burger cook, and someone who dresses the meat. Special orders disrupt the assembly line process by requiring special handling. As a result, most kitchen help at the burger shops purposely take longer with special orders to discourage the patron from ever making a special order again. Fish and chicken specials are worse than hamburgers because they take so much longer to cook. The cooks purposely start off new with these orders. Since chicken takes about 1½ minutes and fish requires 4 minutes, your wait is extended.

■ DEALING WITH THE POST OFFICE

I wanted to include a section on the post office before it discontinues itself right out of business. The postal service ranks up there with the utilities and oil companies as the organization we most love to hate. Yet 18 cents (even 20 cents) is still a cheap way to send information when compared to the time and gasoline costs of taking something to its destination or to the rates of a long-distance phone call. Mail gives us something to be curious about and is the highlight of many people's day.

● *Minimize Your Unwanted Mail*

If only there was a way to get rid of all that junk mail! One of my pet peeves is being sent an advertisement with postage due. Surprisingly, many postal patrons are unaware that they have the right to refuse unwanted mail. All you need do is write "refused" on the unopened envelope and stick it back in the mailbox for the carrier to pick up. I regularly refuse all junk mail. This is better than throwing it away since many firms remove unproductive names from their lists to save future mailing costs.

● *Stop Junk Mail at the Source*

Every time you subscribe to any magazine, send for information, or request a credit card you are putting your name and address on the open market. When you give your name out for *any* purpose, use a different middle initial. Keep track of which initial was used where. Then when you begin to get junk mail you can identify who sold or gave out your name. Then write that organization requesting they stop distributing your name and address.

● *Punish Junk Mailers*

It's petty and vindictive, but so psychologically satisfying. Mail back all return-postage-paid envelopes empty. The mailer runs an account with the post office and is billed postage and a per piece surcharge by volume received. This won't get you off a list but generates a feeling of retribution. If you are really nasty, throw enough scrap paper into the envelope so that it weighs over an ounce. This will cost the junk mailer extra postage if it is caught.

● *Use the Junk Mailer's Envelopes*

If you want to take the time to open junk mail, it is a great source of free envelopes. Sometimes the address portion is left blank as is the return portion. If the address portion is preprinted, you can buy a box of blank mailing label stickers for a few dollars and use the stickers to cover the address portion. Or if ugly isn't a problem, you can cross out the preprinted address and write in the one you want. Please don't do this using postpaid envelopes without a stamp. It's against the law to mail for free on other people's money. Cover up the mailing permit box with a stamp.

● Use Substation Post Offices

Generally, the larger the post office, the more crowded. If you can get to a smaller substation, the lines are short or nonexistent. Also, post office boxes are cheaper and more available.

● Use Special USPO Rates

The post office has several alternatives that the public may utilize to save money:

1. Third class rate. This is for packages weighing less than a pound. It's about the cheapest way you can send a package providing you don't want it insured and don't mind the slower delivery.

2. Library rate. This rate offers you a cheap way to return books to any public or university library. When compared to the cost of gasoline and time, it can also save you money. The current rates show you how inexpensive this service is: 17 cents for up to one pound, 6 cents for each additional pound to seven pounds, 5 cents each pound thereafter.

3. AO (other articles) international rate. This rate is reserved for parcels under two pounds and printed matter under four pounds. Rates vary by country, but usually run 50 percent or less than the parcel post rates for a small package.

● *Alternatives to the USPO*

Competition has sprung up where the law allows and where the USPO is particularly costly or slow.

1. United Parcel Service. The dark brown UPS trucks are a familiar sight on most streets. The UPS is cheaper, faster, and safer than the USPO. UPS requires a signature on delivery and is easier to deal with on insurance claims. The UPS's Blue Ribbon Service compares favorably with the USPO's Priority Mail airmail delivery service by delivering parcels airmail faster and cheaper. For $2 the UPS will even pick up items at your home for a week. The only restriction with UPS is that you can send to street addresses only.

2. Next bus out. If a package must get to another city quickly, you can ship it on the next bus connecting with the destination. There is no pickup or delivery, so you must take it to the bus station and have the parcel picked up at the other end.

3. Next flight out. Almost all the airline companies have parcel services allowing you to ship parcels on the next flight connecting with the destination. Once again, you must deliver the parcel and have it picked up at the other end. For shorter distances, both the next bus and flight out services are normally faster than the USPO's Express Mail, but also more costly.

■ PEAK PATTERNS FOR A VARIETY OF SERVICES

The following services have business patterns which can help you know when to avoid busy times. Here they are in no special order:

1. Libraries. Libraries are more crowded in the evenings because of students. Rather than go to the library for information, call the reference desk and see if someone can look it up for you. This is another example of your tax dollar at work, so they are always glad to help you—their patron.

2. Cleaners. Their slowest season is midsummer. Take your winter coats and suits in around July and get them back quickly. Nothing is worse than being surprised by an early cold spell, then digging your coat out only to find you look like Willy the Chimney Sweep from *Mary Poppins.*

3. Nursing homes. There is no real pattern to nursing home applications. The best sign of a good home is a waiting list. If there is no list, you might try to find out what other people know that you don't.

4. Diaper service. There is never a shortage of diapers. Sometimes the summertime is slower for them since many people prefer to home wash diapers and hang them out to dry.

5. Massage parlor. They cater primarily to traveling businessmen, so Monday through Thursday are their busiest days. They can schedule about two men per hour per masseuse. Busy times are 1:00 P.M. to 2:00 A.M. Calling then

means a several hour wait. Business is slowest in the early evening hours. Business is better in the wintertime, particularly for the out-call service, since men are less willing to leave their hotel rooms. Christmas is the slowest season.

6. Television rental. Fridays and Saturdays are extremely busy. Demand is fairly even all year except around football playoff time. People want to see the bowl games and playoff games on a decent TV.

7. Printing. The three summer months are slowest because of vacations and reduced advertising of businesses. There is the smallest back-up at this time.

8. Beauty shop. There are no significant seasonal variations. Monday and Tuesday are the slowest days. Women begin getting ready for the weekend later in the week. Several shops reported that they were less busy between 11:00 A.M. and 1:00 P.M. during the important "soap operas."

9. Barber. The slow day for barbers is Thursday. You can count the individual hairs on the floor then. Saturdays look like an orphanage commercial.

10. Television repair. The slowest season is the beginning of summer when people don't care to stay inside. The busiest time begins in September and continues through the Super Bowl as men race to see whether their sets or their eyes will burn out first.

11. Mortuaries. Nobody wants to plan needing this service, but it has patterns, too. Most mortuaries refuse to give their employees vacations during August or January. August is the hottest month of the year and causes deaths. January is the coldest, which has the same result. Plus all the older people hanging on for one more Christmas let go after the holidays. Post-Christmas depression claims additional victims.

12. Laundromats. The tubs are busiest evenings and weekends. The best times of day are during the soap operas around lunch or right before mealtime when most homemakers are fixing dinner.

13. Dog grooming. Friday and Saturday are always busy, while Wednesday is the least booked. Business slows down around the start of school in late August and early September and slows down again at Christmastime. Spring tends to be fairly busy as many owners prepare their pets for the summer.

14. Movers. Schedule a van line early if you plan to move in the summer. May to September is frantic for the moving industry. The end of each month is another peak because people move when their lease is up. Mondays and Fridays are also heavy as people plan their move around a weekend.

15. Tuxedo rental. January and February are the slowest months. Some smaller rental places experience problems keeping up with demand during prom time, so you want to reserve ahead of time. As an interesting side note,

several longtime rental stores mentioned that more weddings have been canceled the last two years than ever before. The woman used to be the one who backed out, but now the men are changing their minds and walking out in record numbers.

16. Plumbers. No time seems to be very good for getting plumbers. Their busiest day is Monday since the Law of the Perversity of Inanimate Objects predicts that things always break on weekends. Wednesday and Thursday are the slowest for plumbers.

There are many other services that could be listed, but they show the same busy or slack patterns. In general, Monday and Friday are the two worst business days for almost any service. Midweek, midmorning, and midafternoon are the best times. When in doubt, call ahead and see how the crowd is flowing.

"Thank God the telephone wasn't invented by Alexander Graham Siren!"

–George Carlin

6

Up Close and Personal

I can't think of anyone I'd rather see helped than me. After I was born to win, I deactivated my erroneous zones, pulled my own strings, became my best friend, decided I'm okay, dressed for success, and looked out for No. 1 while watching my body language through the passages of life. But enough is enough. "Me" has had more attention lately than Charlie's Angels in boot camp. Now is the time to learn how to deal with several personal items more conveniently and successfully. And one of the most common personal tools is the telephone.

■ BREAKING FREE OF TELEPHONE SLAVERY

I continue to be amazed at what people will *stop* doing to answer the telephone. "Oh, you were doing WHAT? Well, don't get mad at me. Why in the hell did you answer it anyway?"

Most of us don't have our curiosity well enough in control to keep from answering the phone. Each ring signals an opportunity for excitement, heartwarming communication, a rip-off sales pitch. It's too bad we can't be like the New England store owner who calmly wrote up a customer's order while a phone rang insistently only two feet away. When the customer remarked about the jangling phone, the storekeeper flatly replied, "I use a phone for *my* convenience, not for *its*."

● *Control Telephone Disruption*

If you aren't the type to ignore a ringing phone no matter how friendly the interpersonal moment or how interesting the final minute of a football game, do your loved one and your love of sports a favor and take care of the phone.

○ *Silence the phone*

If the ring is too jarring, you can purchase a silencer switch which attaches to your phone. These are available at any electronics store. Another way is to have all your extensions installed with four-pronged jacks. You can then create quiet time in a particular room while the phone still rings elsewhere or quiet the whole house. (If no jacks are connected, callers hear the ring as if you were not home.) If you have a newer phone installation, the small plug connectors will work for this. They are not as sturdy as the four-pronged jacks, though, for repeated use.

○ *Use "call forwarding"*

The call forwarding feature is available for users serviced by the Bell family's new ESS (Electronic Switching System) central offices. With it you can automatically have your calls forwarded to another number. This is handy if you are going to be at a friend's and don't wish to miss calls, or if you want to direct your calls to an answering service and don't want to pay for a separate extension.

What one man does is use it as a message service. When he is out of town he sets his call forwarding number to Dial-a-Prayer. If he is in town but not home, the phone rings unanswered. This way his friends know whether to keep trying or to wait until he returns from a trip. You can set up the same type of system with your friends to tell them you are gone or just don't want to be disturbed. If you receive frequent long-distance calls, forward the call to an out-of-service number. This will save the caller the cost of a minimum-connect long-distance charge.

○ *Use a phone answering machine*

Nothing is more irritating than to call long distance and be trapped by a phone answering machine. One of my pet peeves is calling and not realizing it's a machine, then beginning the conversation:

"Hello," I hear.

"Hi, Bob. Listen, do you . . ."

"This is Bob Stuckey speaking to you through my phone answering machine." The droning voice continues, "I'm not here right now. At the time of the tone . . ."

"Augh!" Slam!

Phone answering machines are great ways in theory to not miss any phone calls. The only problem is that only about one third to one fourth of the callers ever leave a message. Normally you get thirty seconds of dial tone on the tape.

You can double the number of people leaving messages by being creative about the answering tape you provide. I began recording funny answering messages each week. One week I thanked the callers and said that as a payment for leaving a message I had copied an excerpt of Nixon's White House tapes for their enjoyment. Silence followed. Another time I played the part of a lonely phone answering machine hungry to be turned on, given a spin, and whispered to so sweetly that I would never forget. My clients and friends loved the messages and left responses in record numbers. The only problem is that after a while I began to get callers who just wanted to hear the recordings. But it beat missing messages.

● *Get Rid of Pesky Callers*

Sometimes you are afflicted with a caller suffering jogger's jaw—running off at the mouth. Other callers selling the types of goods better marketed off the back of a wagon practice chin boogie. While phone selling is no less honorable than other sales professions, sometimes solicitors don't know when to quit. This is when you can be creative in getting off the phone.

○ *Hang up*

Before we get carried away with all sorts of esoteric techniques for phone separation, there is no law that says you have to keep that handset up to the side of your head. For heavy breathers, dirty talkers, diarrhea lips, or pesky salespeople, simply hang up. The tech heavy crowd calls it going "on hook."

○ *Hang up when you're talking*

If you've been trying to end an interminable conversation gracefully and have failed, simply hang up when YOU'RE talking. Don't return the handset to the cradle or your voice will fade away. Just reach over and push the cradle button. This will give a good, clean break. No one will believe that anyone would hang up on themselves. Afterward, keep the phone off hook for a moment so your line will busy out if the other person dials. They will assume you are trying to call back and hang up to wait. With any luck someone else will call them or they will be distracted and forget about calling you again.

○ *Crinkle cellophane*

If you have a flair for the dramatic, you can use the cellophane approach. One businessman keeps a large piece of cellophane by his phone for long-distance calls. When he can't end a conversation gracefully, he begins crinkling the cellophane near the mouthpiece and moves the handset away from his ear. As his voice fades he says, "I'm getting a lot of noise on the line. I can't hear you. If you can hear me, thanks for talking. I'll call again soon." Clunk.

○ *Screen salespeople with the listing*

A radio interviewer has a unique approach for immediately identifying phone solicitors. Her directory listing has her last name spelled backward. For example, she would be listed under: Joan M. Smailliw (not her real name). When her friends ask for her number, she reminds them that it's in the phone book under her last name spelled backward. This is so unusual they never forget. So when she receives calls asking for Ms. Smailliw, she knows automatically it isn't a friend and she can immediately brush them off. Her favorite brushoff is to say, "She's dead. I'm the second wife and I just don't want to talk about her." Clunk.

● *Get Rid of Rude or Abusive Callers*

Some salespeople can't take a "No" and some obscene callers love to hear anything. There are lots of fun ways to get rid of bill collectors, insensitive salespeople, or sickies:

○ *Lay the phone down*

A bill collector told me the most effective method used against him was to lay the phone down and walk away. If the caller keeps bothering you, just say "Just one moment please" and set the phone down. Then go turn on a good made-for-TV movie and listen for the phone off-hook beeping.

○ *Learn a foreign sentence*

Everyone needs to know at least one sentence of a foreign language, preferably something like Mandarin or Ubangi. Answer the phone with the neutrally accented, "Allo?" then reel off your gibberish when the sales spiel starts: "Qeeumska labanie topah soptah sacta peyuma quiatopah grabswa—sowinksah grabswa" (the numbers one to ten in Osage Indian). This really swings with normal voice inflections and a speedy delivery.

○ *It's against your religion*

Tell the persistent solicitor it's against your religion. We gave old clothes and some furniture to a charitable organization once. Now we are besieged by calls demanding to know why we don't have anything again. It's currently "against my religion" to give to these people. Slowly but surely we're getting off the lists.

○ *Claim to rent*

If the solicitor is selling anything for the home, say you rent. With the current real estate market, more and more people are renting homes so this is quite typical.

○ *You had it done last week*

What a coincidence! Every time you're called about having something done to the home, tell them you had it done last week. Always thank those nice people for calling, but remind them you won't be in the market for such goods for many years now and suggest they take you off their list.

○ *You've been out of work for a month*

Nothing scares off a pushy salesperson like hearing you're a bad debt waiting to happen. Express interest in the idea, but explain that you've been out of work for a month and would have to give serious thought before buying anything. The solicitor won't be able to get the button down fast enough.

○ *Your brother sells it*

I've made an informal study and had others verify the results. Particularly with insurance salespeople who seem to be unable to comprehend the word NO, explain that your *brother* sells the product. Every relationship has been tried: father, mother, sister, in-laws, cousin, etc., but brother gets the best results. They just won't sell against a brother.

● *Discourage Obscene or Prank Callers*

All the troublesome caller wants is to generate a little interpersonal communication. A gasp of horror or disgust will suffice. Actual statements of revulsion are ecstasy. Anger is fun, too. What you must do is remove the payoff, because this caller may not be stopped by hanging up.

○ *Hang up immediately*

The first try is to hang up as fast as possible. Don't bang the phone down or even that will give some small measure of satisfaction. This may generate some return calls, but if you are persistent the caller may give up due to lack of feedback.

○ *Forward the call*

If you are bothered by persistent harassment, use your call forwarding feature immediately after the first call. There is nothing a sickie wants to hear less than, "Police station, 15th District." Forwarding an obscene call to Dial-a-Prayer or to the time and temperature number is also providing a useful service to the caller. Then you are unreachable. (If you don't have call forwarding, answer in a different voice with "State Highway Patrol." Oops!)

○ *Use a police whistle*

A first-class police whistle is an ideal way to pay back the obscene caller for his abuse. A solid blast can be enough to break his eardrum on the other end. This is a bit severe for a prankster, so use this only on the truly obnoxious sickies.

○ Get a "trap"

The telephone company should be notified if you are being harassed regularly on the phone. Their engineers can put a "trap" on the line to locate where the obscene call originates. Call your customer service representative for information.

○ Pretend someone is listening

One woman stopped a series of troublesome phone calls by loosely covering up the mouthpiece during one of them and saying loudly, "Did you get all that, Sergeant?" With any luck you can put a nice scare into a persistent prankster.

● Get Through the Screening Secretary

Many times persons fail to reach the phone before it stops ringing. The phone company recommends letting the phone ring ten times on the other end before hanging up. This offers the best chance of giving the person enough time to reach the phone. But often your problem isn't one of getting the phone answered or finding an open line, it's one of fighting through the screening secretary. Here are some ideas:

○ State the call is person-to-person

With the advent of male operators, anyone can call and tell the secretary the call is person-to-person. After all, it IS person-to-person. You don't need to lie and say it's long distance. The secretary will assume you are an operator and may put you through. Once in with the boss, you can converse as if the secretary had put you through locally.

○ *Refer to the person by first name or nickname*

If you are calling a Robert A. Smith, ask jovially for "Bob." If you seek a Charles B. Jones ask for "Chuck" or "Charlie." You don't have much to lose by taking a chance. Sound very casual as if you are old friends. If the secretary asks your name, tell her, "Aw, c'mon. Don't give me that business rigmarole, just let me talk to him." Then when you reach him go back to "Mr. Jones . . ."

○ *Make up a nickname*

If the name doesn't fit a normal nickname (what do you call Elsworth?), try making one up and bluff it out. "Hey, is The Poacher in? . . . You didn't know? Watch him play doubles sometime and you'll see where he picked that up. Let me speak to him . . . Hello, Mr. Jones? My name is . . ."

○ *Put yourself in the best perspective*

A manager for a large appliance firm told me he had about five different business cards. He had cards billing him as sales manager, regional sales manager, sales representative, district sales manager, and vice president of sales. Whenever he met a new customer, he felt out the customer for what level of sales executive he wanted to be called on by. The appliance company didn't care as long as sales were up.

Treat yourself the same way. A reporter for a small radio station always calls explaining he's from CBS (the station is a CBS affiliate). Other reporters are not above saying they are from Walter Cronkite's or

Jessica Savitch's staff. I prefer to put myself in the best light. I'm not self-employed; I am president of my one-man company. "President" gets better results.

● Complain by Phone

The phone is a great tool to save trips. Let your fingers do the walking. Don't go shopping without making certain by phone that the item is in stock. The same works for complaining. Try to solve the problem by phone first before investing in a trip.

○ Always get the person's name and location

Any time you call an organization FOR ANY REASON, get the name of the person you're dealing with. Keep a pad by your phone and quickly write the name down when the call is answered. If in doubt, make a point of having the person spell out the name so that it is clear you will be back if there are further problems. When you've been transferred from another extension, get the new number so you can dial directly in next time.

○ Summarize and repeat everything

After you have gotten a response to your problem, positive or negative, summarize your explanation of the problem, repeat the response, and then repeat the name. "Now, you understand that the auto speed control picks up with an uncomfortable lurch and that I feel it's out of adjustment from the installation. You're telling me that you won't readjust it at no cost since it's been on the road for two weeks. And your name is Joan Doe. Fine, Joan. I'm going to be following up on this with someone higher up and I wanted to make certain everything is clear." You will be surprised how little bottlenecks tend to suddenly break free after one of these statements.

○ *Keep coming back to the same person*

When you are getting musical phones, i.e., being directed from department to department, you have made a mistake with the first person. When you are shifted off to someone else, remind the first person that should the second person not be of help, you will be getting back. "Okay I talked to Jim over in accounting and he didn't help. He said it was the controller's function. So I thought I'd come back to you. Who should I see now?" Once the person decides that you will never go away until the problem is solved, you won't be sent on any more wild-goose chases.

○ *Intimidate an abusive caller*

If you are being browbeaten by someone over the phone and have their name, ask to speak to the manager immediately. Stay calm and repeat what has been said to you with the statement, "I thought you would want to know what is happening. I can't believe *this* is how you want your customers treated." If there isn't a manager to appeal to, interrupt the person's tirade and state, "I've just turned on my tape recorder. I believe by law I have to inform you that I'm now taping the conversation and your last remarks have been recorded. Now if you want to, continue with what you have to say. I wanted it on record." Whether you are actually taping or not is up to you. (Carrying a tape recorder into any meeting where you think someone will get abusive is a great intimidation tactic. Its mere presence will keep things calm.)

● *Get Faster Phone Service*

If you are in need of faster phone service and the repairman hasn't come or else you can't live with the lead time, keep calling every hour or so. The phone company keeps detailed performance statistics on its central offices and rates the personnel accordingly. You will be messing up the central office performance figures by generating an exorbitant amount of trouble tickets. Suddenly they will be only too happy to get someone over there before you blast the performance stats beyond recovery.

● *Minimize Your Phone Bill*

A recent landmark court decision cleared the way for telephone company competitors to offer long-distance service. At this time there are two firms offering separate long-distance service, the most prominent of which is MCI. They offer long-distance rates 40 percent or more lower than AT&T to many of the nation's larger cities. There is currently a flat monthly fee in addition to the calling charges, but MCI advertises that if your long-distance bill is at least $25 per month you will likely save money. An advantage of MCI is that you can use it from a push-button phone and still have it billed to you. A disadvantage is that MCI covers only selected cities (the list is growing all the time).

● *Call When You Are Most Likely to Find the Party In*

Southwestern Bell Telephone publishes a booklet entitled, *The Bell Guide to Getting More Done by Long*

Distance. In it is reproduced a long-distance call timing chart developed by Mutual of New York. A copy of this table below gives you a guide for timing your long-distance calls to the audience.

Prospects	*Best Time to Call*
Chemists and engineers	Between 4 P.M. and 5 P.M.
Clergymen	Thursday or Friday
Contractors and builders	Before 9 A.M. or after 5 P.M.
Dentists	Before 9:30 A.M.
Druggists and grocers	Between 1 P.M. and 3 P.M.
Executive and business heads	After 10:30 A.M.
Housewives	Between 10 A.M. and 11 A.M.
Lawyers	Between 11 A.M. and 2 P.M.
Merchants, stores heads, and department heads	After 10:30 A.M.
Physicians and surgeons	Between 9 A.M. and 11 A.M.; after 4 P.M.
Professors and schoolteachers	At home, between 6 P.M. and 7 P.M.
Public accountants	Anytime during the day, but avoid January 15 through April 15.
Publishers and printers	After 3 P.M.
Small-salaried people and government employees	Call at home.
Stockbrokers and bankers	Before 10 A.M. or after 3 P.M.
Prospects, at home	Monday nights between 7 P.M. and 9 P.M.

Source: Mutual of New York.

TIMING LONG-DISTANCE CALLS.
Table 6-1

■ FINDING A JOB

I ran a résumé service part-time for about five years before becoming a professional speaker. During that period, I spent my evenings and weekends writing résumés and counseling people on how to handle themselves during interviews. The advice I sold was the result of interviewing several hundred executives concerning how they handled job applications and what applicants were evaluated on. My later experience verified what they told me—very few people know how to find a job properly and efficiently. What follows regularly sold for $50 per hour:

● *Get Interviews from Every Source You Can*

The mistake many people make is in depending upon a single source to find a job. They scan the newspaper ads each Sunday or they go to an agency figuring a good agent will know about any available jobs. What you want is the same type of system Nature designed for the plant and animal world—throw out millions of seeds and be content when one or two make good. Your job-finding program should utilize every available source.

○ *Answer promising newspaper advertisements*

The Sunday employment pages are one of the most competitive places to look for a job. They also offer the best potential for succeeding because most of the applicants do such a lousy job. You can stand out from the crowd easily by understanding the system:

　　1. Don't reply to an ad immediately. I placed an advertisement for a researcher to help with this

book and received 150 calls on Monday. Tuesday I received about 70, Wednesday about 10, and then only a trickle for another few days or so. The response to written ads runs about the same. Delay your reply at least a week to ten days. It's the same buying principle as the used car. If the job was filled right away, you probably wouldn't have gotten it anyway. By applying late, your résumé will be hitting the decision-maker when the field has been narrowed down to the finalists. By avoiding the crowd you have a better likelihood of having your information read. Finally, even if you are underqualified the requirements may not have been met and the employer may be willing to ease up on the requirements.

2. Send a cover letter with a résumé. In ads I've placed, only about one in ten respondents enclosed both a cover letter and résumé. Some sent letters only, some just the résumé. You want to stand out. The résumé is general, the cover letter points out why you match the specific needs of the ad. The cover letter should include where and what day you saw the ad (the company may have several running in many different cities), what position you are applying for (it might have 100 job searches going at once), and then explain why you are right for the job.

3. Follow up in two weeks. Only one person in 200 ever bothered to follow up after the initial letter to remind me they were still interested in the research job. Give it a second shot. Your résumé might have been lost, overlooked, or rejected. Most employers are impressed by

someone with persistence and drive. In my case, I hired the woman who followed up. She was the only one who applied who proved she truly wanted the job.

○ *Use employment agencies carefully*

There are about as many snakes in the employment business as in any "body shop" type of operation. Some places treat you like meat on a hook—you keep expecting Rocky Balboa to jog by and start punching on you. Other places are grateful for your business and the opportunity to place you.

1. Shop carefully for an employment agency. Check with the Better Business Bureau before you apply anywhere. Find out if others have had problems there. If you get an interview with a company and are rejected for the job, call back and ask the interviewer which agency their firm respects the most, that you wish to find a competent agent. Talk to friends who have used an agency and see what they have to say.

2. Apply at only one agency. The worst thing that can happen is to let several employment agencies have your name and begin plastering it all over town. Obviously the agencies use many of the same client companies. So when a prospective employer sees your name coming from two directions, he will back off. You are nothing more than a potential problem, because no matter who he contacts first, the other agency who has your name will be unhappy. Another advantage of limiting agency listings is that your name is in their file forever. A listing with items

like salary history can suddenly get back on the market at a later date and embarrass you. That's why it's good to request in writing that the agency remove your application information from the file after you have obtained a job. You have no guarantee it will be done, but at least you have asked.

3. Contact them at the right time. Mondays are terribly busy at agencies. The end of the working day is also hectic because employers tend to call late afternoon with job listings. Early afternoon is normally the slowest part of the day.

4. Remember you're doing the agency a favor. Employment agencies intimidate the applicant into becoming another one of the sheep being fed into the shearing system. Never forget that they are going to make money because of *you*. They are not doing you any favor. You are profit waiting to happen. For example, I never filled out their application forms. I gave them my résumé and said to the receptionists, "Here is my background. I'm not going to take my time to fill out the form when it might turn out you can't help me. Give this to Mr. Salami instead."

● *Stand Out in the Interview Process*

Once again job applicants go through the interview process with no thought as to standing out from the crowd. Proper interviews are well-planned events in which you have the opportunity to sell yourself.

1. Know who you will see. When an interview is scheduled, ask who you will be meeting. After

the first interview, you will often speak to several people who will make a group decision on you. BEFORE THE INTERVIEW send a brief letter with a copy of your résumé telling each person how interested you are in the job and how much you're looking forward to speaking with them. I guarantee it will be the first time it's ever happened to them. It's the type of special touch that impresses.

2. Bring a packet for each person at the interview. The personnel department has professional interviewers. When you are to talk to someone in the department where you may be working, you often have the manager with the lowest seniority who has been stuck with the job. Don't depend on the manager having your résumé and application for the interview. Bring a copy for each person you will see, just in case.

3. Take notes. You don't want to take copious records of the conversation. Just jot down key points you have been told about the job. Record any favorable comments you are given and any reservations the person may have about you. Get down a few key facts for later use, and get the spellings of names correct.

4. Ask for the job. At the end of interview, ask for the job! It's a crime to sit there and trade facts, then not care enough to say, "I want the job." At the end state, "I know you will be getting together with the other people I'm meeting today. But at this point, what is your feeling? I'm very interested in working for Allied Allies. Do you think I'm the person you're looking for?" You may get a "Yes," you may hear some

hemming and hawing. But you will have positively asked for the job. If you hear a "No," then you have bought one last chance to sell yourself. Without asking, you would have had no chance.

5. Write follow-up letters. The evening of the interviews, write a follow-up letter to each and every person you spoke with. Comment on some of the facts from the interview, thank the person for any positive comments, and restate your desire to win the job. Once again, this will be the first time the executive has ever received this. You will appear infinitely more professional than anyone else going for the job. There is no guarantee, of course, but your odds for getting the job will be greatly improved.

● *Develop a Good Résumé*

There have always been arguments over what is the best formula for a résumé. In interviewing executives, I found an overwhelming preference for a one-page résumé. You don't want to pass a security check, you want to create just enough interest for the executive to wish to meet you. You also want to provide a quick reference for someone unprepared during the job interview.

The résumé format illustrated in Figure 6-2 achieves all these goals. Any good reference book from the library will tell you what to put in each section. Executives tend to scan résumés for specific "hot buttons." These vary from interviewer to interviewer, so all you can hope to do is make any section readily accessible. As you can see, the résumé shown accomplishes this.

RÉSUMÉ
name
address
city, state zip
(area) phone

JOB OBJECTIVE: _____
_____
_____
_____

PERSONAL DATA: Age _____ Height _____
Status—married/single Weight _____

EDUCATION: _____
_____
_____

COLLEGE HONORS
& ACTIVITIES: _____
_____
_____
_____

PROFESSIONAL
ACTIVITIES: _____
_____
_____

EXPERIENCE: company   job title
city, state month 19___ to present
_____
_____
_____

company
city, state job title
month 19___ to month 19 ___
_____
_____
_____

company
city, state job title
month 19___ to month 19 ___
_____
_____
_____

company
city, state job title
month 19___ to month 19 ___
_____
_____

FIGURE 6-2

Have your résumé printed. There is no need to have it typeset. This smacks of a professional's touch and can turn the executive off. But a résumé printed professionally on high quality paper attracts attention. Also use an off-white or light shade of pastel color. (Stay away from bright colors; they look like cheap fliers.) I've always preferred a faint tan color. Imagine a desk littered with several hundred resumes and cover letters. The nonwhite high quality paper stands out immediately. If you think there are so many people being interviewed that there will be trouble remembering your face, include a professionally shot photo on the résumé. If not, omit a picture. It may hurt you.

As with so many of the insider's tips, you need to stand out from the crowd by being a little bit smarter about what goes on behind the scenes. Keep seeing yourself and the job-hunting process from the eyes of an interviewer. Once you understand the volume of replies and the problems associated with picking one person out of this mess, you will understand the value of standing out.

■ MISCELLANY

There were a number of items which didn't fit into any particular personal category but were too deserving to leave out. In no order of importance are more ideas:

● *Left-Handers' Information*

If you are the one person in ten who knows that it's no fun being left-handed in a right-handed world, then this item is for you. What you may need is a membership in the *International Left-Handers Society*. For a $10 membership fee you receive typical goodies such as a plaque, card, T-shirt, newsletter subscription, and most importantly, a guide to lefty products. Write: ILHS, Box 10198, Milwaukee, WI 53210.

If you need a little cheering up about being left-handed, you might try your library for a copy of *The Left-Handed Book* by James T. deKay. This is a fun little book that takes only a few minutes to read and passes out practical advice such as: Eat left and let the other customers at the lunch counter work it out. If a tool at work is right-handed, try a rest break until a left-handed version is developed. DeKay also urges lefties to demand a Bill of Lefts, to support baseball because it favors lefties, and to support only left-handed artists.

If you are looking for left-handed products such as scissors, pen, knife, soup ladle, special how-to books, or whatever, there is hope. Try your Yellow Pages or contact: The Left Hand, 140 W. 22nd St., New York, NY 10011. Their catalog is available for only $1, which is applicable toward any subsequent purchase. Another source is The Sinister Shop, 71 McCul, Toronto, ONT. M5T 2X1, Canada. Finally you won't need to break your wrist trying to wind your watch again.

● *The Most Accurate Clock*

John Luckman wrote in an issue of the Gamblers Book Club *Overlay* newsletter about how book-makers use the nation's most accurate clock. If a bookie's clock is slow, he is open to some gypster placing a late bet *after the results are known*. This is called "past-posting" (remember Robert Shaw in *The Sting*?). Bookmakers avoid this scam by synchronizing to the Master Clock at the U.S. Naval Observatory in Washington, D.C. Its number is (202) 254-4950.

Upon dialing the above number, you'll hear a ticking background sound with a male voice calmly reciting: "U.S. Naval Observatory Master Clock. At the tone, Eastern Standard Time: X hours, X minutes, X seconds. (beep) Universal Time: X hours, X minutes, X seconds. (beep) U.S. Naval Observatory. . ." The whole cycle takes fifteen seconds with the E.S.T. announced after ten seconds and the Universal Time five seconds later to allow an interval for the announcement. This repeats four times so that you can synchronize to any part of the minute before being automatically cut off.

The E.S.T. is given in terms of a twenty-four-hour clock so that you'll have to convert back to twelve-hour time. For example, 15 hours, 38 minutes, 10 seconds converts to 10 seconds after 3:38 P.M. You'll also have to convert to the appropriate time zone if you don't live in the E.S.T. zone. Universal Time is often called Greenwich Time (the Universal Time Master Clock is located in Greenwich, England) and is the standard time referred to for international communications. From now on, you need never wonder, "What time is it?"

● *Getting Called On in a Crowd*

If there was to be the least important tip in the book, this would be a front-runner for the title. Nonetheless, the silly thing works. The next time you are at a meeting or in a class wanting to be called on, waving your hand futilely, try this trick. Instead of waving with an open palm like the "How" sign, or pointing a finger up in the air, make the okay sign with your thumb and first finger. For some reason, the unusual hand position seems to attract the speaker's attention from the many other hands in the crowd and you will be called on. Try it.

"The nearest thing to immortality in this world is a government bureau."
—*Gen. Hugh S. Johnson*

7

Grappling with the Government

I had great hopes for this chapter. If there is a single entity in all the world that could benefit from easier, faster, and cheaper, it must be the U.S. federal government. There should be an entire book full. With bated breath I sent the researcher off to begin probing the "giant run by pygmies." On each radio appearance, I highlighted the government as one of the prime targets of the book. If ever there was a system that needed to be beaten, this was it.

We uncovered a few tips, most of which were generic to any organizational bureaucracy. We were told to write our representatives in Congress and hope that they had an efficient constituent service program. It was suggested that the government bureaucrats worked if you kept at them until they made you go away by doing what you wanted. But there were no real zingers which people who understood the government could use to slice through the red tape and get things done.

Over the last twenty or so radio interviews, I mentioned I had no specific government tips and challenged the listeners to call in with their special hint. Host after host bragged, "MY listeners will help you out. We've surely got *someone* out there who can beat the government system." The phones stayed silent.

The conclusion is that if you get thrown into the government bureaucracy, make certain your will is up to date. We couldn't find ONE hint that related *specifically* to the government. Evidently, A always comes before B, comes before C. Heaven help you if you need to go from A to D. Getting people to do their job is one thing common to any group, but cutting government corners seems to be unknown. I can't believe the hints don't exist. But whoever knows them is in a select group.

"Wealthy person: Someone who always buys a bargain."

–Anonymous

8

Consume or Be Consumed

Money wouldn't be such a problem if we didn't have to spend it all the time. I've always felt that my mistake in life was not in the way I've lived, but that I was given the wrong name at birth. I should have been an Onassis, a Getty, or a Rockefeller. These are names that end up on office buildings, that consume rather than are consumed. They accomplish it with sheer magnitude of the trading stamps of life, money.

The rest of us mortals must use a bit of subterfuge. As consumers (rather than those who consume) we must make do with money as a limited resource.

■ HANDLING CREDIT

Credit is nothing more complex than Wimpy offering, "I will gladly pay you tomorrow for a hamburger today." The obtain now–purchase later plan is both a benefit and a trap. The benefit is that we can acquire goods immediately and save money in an inflationary economy, and the trap is that we can obtain now without ever *being able* to save the money. One is good money management, the other is financial quicksand.

● *Ask for a Cash Discount*

When you charge an item, the seller pays a percentage of the total purchase price to the charge card company. The amount paid varies upon the volume of transactions given to the company and the average ticket price. A dentist told me he pays a 2 percent fee. This is low because his average charge ticket is considered a large amount. A retail store with a smaller per ticket amount may pay as much as 5 to 7 percent.

The seller must build this discount into the prices. So the cash purchasers are paying higher prices because of the credit card buyers. Consumer groups have been arguing for years that this is unfair to the cash buyer. If you are in a smaller store, ask the salesperson if there is a discount for cash since there will be no credit card service charge incurred. You may save as much as 7 percent off the list price if the seller passes this savings on to you.

● *Retain All Charge Card Receipts*

Be careful to retain all charge card receipts and compare them to your bill at the end of the month. We were vacationing in Florida one summer and were nearly cheated out of $50 by a motel. I paid the bill with American Express and as usual filed the receipt away. When my statement came weeks later, the motel bill was $50 higher than I had signed for. I examined the receipt returned with the bill and found that the amount had been changed with a handwritten note on the bill, "Amount changed in front of customer."

Fortunately, I had the receipt copy showing the amount had *not* been changed on my receipt. I contacted American Express, sent them a copy of the receipt, and had the fraudulent amount removed from my bill. Without the receipt, I would have been unable to prove my claim.

● *Check Your Card After Each Use*

It's not uncommon for credit cards to get switched by accident, especially in a restaurant or other places where several cards are being run through the machine at any one time. Instead of putting your card back in your wallet without a glance, check your card to make certain it's yours. In addition, check your card to make certain it has been signed. A dishonest merchant or a thief can find an unsigned card and switch another card for it; then, if you don't notice, use it with a completely matching signature.

● *Keep Track of Purchases*

A danger of credit card convenience is that you generally have no idea how much money you are spending. The card smoothly changes hands many times over the course of a month and suddenly you are faced with a $500 charge bill costing you $7.50 this month. Most money management experts suggest you keep a small note card in your wallet and record each time you make a credit purchase. Simply enter the date, amount, and the running total of all purchases since the last payment. This way you will know exactly how much your total debt is at any point in time and can make a purchase decision accordingly.

● *Keep Your Credit Lines to a Minimum*

Many loan officers consider your credit line as an *actual debt* when evaluating your financial position, reasoning that you have the ability to get that much further in debt at any time. The officer assumes the worst case in looking at your debt handling ability. So keep your line of credit no higher than absolutely necessary if you intend to borrow money for other purposes. If the credit card company automatically raises your limit, then write to have it lowered to its original amount.

● *Time Purchases for Maximum Use of Money*

Bankers use a financial concept called "float." Every day your money is in an interest bearing account (like a NOW account for a savings account), it is earning you money. The time between the purchase date of an item and the day money is withdrawn from your account to pay is called "float." Float is beneficial because you not only have use of the item, you are still earning interest on the payment. The longer the float the better.

Most credit cards charge interest on the amount not paid on the bill immediately following a purchase. Get to know the billing dates for your credit cards. The closing date for bills will consistently be during a certain day of the month. Then, for maximum float, especially when buying large ticket items, make your purchase right after the closing date so the amount will appear on the succeeding month's bills.

The bill states the "pay by" date to avoid additional finance charges. Make the payment immediately before the "pay by" date. For example, assuming the closing date is the 1st of every month, you might buy a $750 refrigerator on the 2nd. This will not appear on your bill until the following month. Assuming you have twenty-five days after closing until interest is charged, you can then send in a check on the 22nd (just to be on the safe side). The check is then presented to your bank for payment the 25th. Your money will be earning interest in your account a total of fifty-three days *after* you purchased the refrigerator. This earns you about $6 in interest you would have lost had you paid cash.

■ GETTING COMPUTER BILLING ERRORS FIXED

Computers are promoted as a boon to mankind. They handle brain-numbing details at the speed of light while freeing human minds and hands for more valuable tasks such as working out the office football pool or phoning home to see if the walls are still standing.

They also propagate human errors on input at truly blinding speeds. And once a computer is programmed to send a bill, it will send it until the last nuclear generator melts down to the earth's core.

Fortunately, the computer is fairly picky about what it likes to eat. Any item that doesn't fit its rigid diet has to be handled by a human operator. This is your big chance. Your only hope of getting a computer billing system to respond to an error is to reach a human somewhere along the line. The secret is to make the computer food indigestible.

● *Punch Holes in the Card*

If you have a billing problem with a system using computer cards *and no one will act on your correspondence*, take a ball-point pen and punch a few extra holes in the card. Then write your message on the card with a red felt-tip pen. The magic fingers of the card reader will have troubles and kick it out. Hopefully, when the operator looks at the card, it will be sorted from the mass handling process and resolved.

● *Shave the Edges of the Card*

If you are in an extravagant mood you can further insure the reader will choke if you cut the edges of the bill card about ¼ inch. Taper them somewhat so that no edge is square with the holes. The magic fingers will line up with the edge of the card and start feeling for holes in the wrong spots. When the card is kicked out, the operator will again see your message emblazoned in red pen.

● *Tape Over the Holes*

A third alternative is to tape over the holes. This turns your card into a nonbill which won't read any information into the computer. Make sure to write your message on the card beforehand, or else you will have problems writing around the tape.

● *Don't Sign Your Payment Check*

You can attack the bill problem from another angle. Make out a check to the company, only don't sign on the bottom line. Instead put your message in red ink. When the company deposits the check, the bank will not honor the invalid signature. Your only concern should be that the bank might honor it anyway.

If you've ever accidentally mixed up the gas and electric payments and switched checks, you may have found out that the checks were cashed even though they were made out to the wrong company. When a utility receives 40,000 checks a day, it doesn't have time to review the "Pay to" line. To protect yourself should you use this check message plan, list the amount as $00.00 in the number box and spell it out on the amount line. Should the check be processed, you won't lose anything.

● *Obliterate the Numbers*

Many companies are using paper bills which are read by an OCR (Optical Character Recognition) reader. You can tell if the bill is OCR-read if it has a large "L" shape (a reference mark) on it or if the number "1" has a little upward curl on the foot. The way to get this rejected in the reading process is to obliterate every number with a wide felt-tip pen. You must use the same color as the print ribbon ink or the reading circuitry will ignore the felt tip. Likewise, merely drawing a line through the characters won't reject the bill. Modern computers are able to interpret the characters based on partial shapes.

● *Staple the Envelope Shut*

If you want to get the bill kicked out earlier in the handling process, you can staple the envelope shut with twenty or thirty staples. Most bills are machine "joggled" to move the bill and check down to the bottom of the envelope, then slit open at the top by machine. If the volume is great enough, a company will also use a machine to "pick" the contents out. By stapling the envelope shut, you make someone take time to open it by hand and examine the contents.

● *Send It to an Executive*

If you still can't get relief, then send a complaint package to an executive. Don't use the bill's return envelope. Payments are usually directed to a special post office box and funneled into the automated system. Send the package to the company's street address. Direct it to the proper executive (it may take a phone call to get a name), and mark the envelope "personal." This will assure that at least the secretary will look at it.

■ HANDLING CONSUMER PROBLEMS

Stores are wonderful examples of applied psychology. At the supermarket the milk and bread are usually located on opposite walls so that you have to walk by the entire store's impulse items at the end of the rows. Elevators and service centers are often in the back of department stores. This way you go by as many departments as possible. The escalators are always arranged so that you must walk around to continue going up or down for the same reason.

A fabric store manager told me that he controls crowds through judicious use of the thermostat. On sales days when his store is overcrowded with shoppers seeking specific items, he lowers the temperature so that the store is a little too cold for comfort. This causes people to do their shopping and leave, making room for others. On regular business days, he keeps the thermostat at a comfortable level so that customers will browse. Given more time in comfort, they tend to buy more.

One store was faced with the problem of too few elevators. During peak periods, customers waited unhappily to move to a different floor. The complaint volume grew until the company commissioned a traffic study to determine how many new elevators were needed. The drawback to adding elevators is that most buildings are not designed to accommodate additional elevator shafts. The cost of adding a shaft is enormous. The store executives felt trapped.

The solution was developed by an industrial psychologist asked by one of the executives to look into the problem. His answer was to install mirrors in the elevator lobbies of each floor. The elevators wouldn't arrive any faster, but people could look at themselves while they waited. The complaints disappeared. The next time you wait for an elevator, see if there isn't a mirror nearby.

Using a little applied psychology is all it takes to handle many consumer problems. Here are a few of the best ideas:

● *Raise Hell*

The first technique is to persistently go after what you want and don't take "No" for an answer. A student once heard her three-year-old say, "Go outside?" to her husband thirty-two times in a row. The boy delivered it in pleading, whining, pitiful, angry, outrageous tones. He garbled a bit and then continued on another nine straight times. At this point the husband screamed, "All right, already, GO

OUTSIDE!" With a merry grin the boy turned and headed out.

Don't be afraid to express how frustrated, angry, disappointed, put out, confused, or stupefied you are. You don't have to apologize for *their* fouling up. They should be helping you.

● *Cry*

A special kind of hell to raise is crying. No man can deal effectively with a crying woman. A woman went to her lawyer about the service runaround she was getting with her new car lemon. She wanted to sue the dealership for the cost of the car. The lawyer accurately advised her that the suit would be prohibitively expensive and that fees would eat up a large chunk of the judgment should she win. His professional advice was that she go down to the showroom on the busiest sales night, Friday, and start crying. She was to loudly wail, "I just don't know what to do anymore. All I get is pushed around and no one will help me . . ." He told her to not move an inch. If anyone tried to usher her out of the showroom into an office, she was to yell, "See, there you go, trying to push me around. You people are so terrible to me . . ."

She couldn't have shut off the sales in that showroom any better had she dragged in a dead skunk. Within minutes her car was on the rack and servicemen were swarming around it. These aren't law school tactics, but they work.

● *Go Up Three Levels*

Some people would argue that you should go right to the top whenever there is a problem. I've found that frequently you end up working with someone in the bottom three levels anyway. Try going from clerk to manager to second-level manager. If that doesn't solve your problem, then go to the top executives with your complaint. Here's why.

A manager in a large retail department store chain told me that store policy on refunds is clearly established. Anyone who goes to the store manager about any problem is automatically given what they want, no matter how outrageous. A woman brought back her twenty-year-old plated silverware for a refund because of teeth marks and chipping. The silver had evidently been used by everyone except Benji. Still, she received her merchandise credit.

This same store will take back *used* ladies' lingerie even though it must be thrown away. Management's philosophy is that anyone mad enough to go from clerk to department manager to store manager should automatically be satisfied. Future business is important enough to warrant losing a little money now to keep a happy customer returning.

● Then Go to the Top

If you haven't gotten satisfaction from the first three levels, then go directly to the top. All companies have procedures for handling the serious complaints that reach the corporate executives. Give them a chance to work.

● Contact the Executive Complaint Department

A business consultant had a serious problem with the local phone company. He bought a new home without phone service. He worked out of his home and moved in only because the phone company promised service within ten days. The ten-day schedule extended to six weeks, then two months, finally three months. After spending weekends unable to contact customers or to receive calls, the consultant began to worry about staying in business. He frantically talked to the phone company service manager, the district engineers, and finally the regional manager. There was still no service to be scheduled soon.

The consultant called the president and explained his problem to the secretary. He told her he would begin a suit to recover damages of lost business caused by the phone company breaking its oral contract. He was immediately given to the Executive Complaint Department. This is where all the serious problems reaching the top executives were handled. It is staffed by old-timers who know the company top to bottom. The consultant's phone was in three days later, even though the district engineer swore there were no available lines.

Since hearing this story, I have had the occasion to call company executives. Now I ask the switchboard operator for the Executive Complaint Department directly and explain that instead of calling the president I sought them out. While the exact name may vary, nearly every large organization has such a group. Call it directly to save time.

● *Fight with Paper*

You will continue to find that "if it isn't written down, it never happened." Fight using the bureaucratic tools, pen and pencil. Send letters. Then send letters talking about how rude they were to ignore your other letters. Get enough letters going until it looks like they are heartless insensitive brutes and you have been more than reasonable. Nothing raises an executive's pulse rate as much as seeing an underling let correspondence regarding a problem slide.

Don't send copies of your letters to other people. It looks as if someone else is handling things. Send a letter referencing what you have done and restate what other letters said if need be.

● Call the Store

If you merely want a question answered, or are having trouble getting someone to help you, go over to a pay phone and call the clerk. This has the same effect as calling the nurses' station in the hospital. Clerks won't do their job, but they'll jump to stop a ringing phone. Get your information, or tell the clerk that since he's not doing anything you'd like some help and will be right over. Remind him to wait for you.

● Work a Little Shock into Your Conversation

If you are getting a runaround over the phone, try for a shock. One man waits until he is asked his phone number and says, "Oh, you can call me at work at the Consumer Protection Office." This seems to make many problems magically disappear. Notice he doesn't claim to be from the Consumer Protection Agency or any other private or governmental agency. This is fraud. He *does* have a CPO, albeit small, which is dedicated to seeing *he* gets a fair deal.

● *Watch Out for Backlash*

A husband called a radio show to tell me about his wife's car. She was always careful in maintaining her car and would insist that the reluctant gas station attendant check the tires for air each time she went in, even if it was on consecutive days. She always went to the same station because of their good service. One day her husband happened to drive the car and noticed it was handling funny. He got out to look it over and noticed the tires seemed unusually round. The right front tire had sixty-four pounds pressure and the left contained eighty-two pounds. The gas station attendant had evidently decided, "If she wants air, she's going to get air." So should you win one in the complaint game, keep alert for backlash because the game isn't over.

■ SAVING TIME WITH MAIL ORDER

I am an avid fan of shopping by mail. The right kind of shopping trip is walking out to the mailbox and back. It saves time, gas, and frequently, money.

● *Use Mail Order for Staples*

Mail order shopping is useful for any staple items like socks, underwear, or name brand items such as tools or toys. Once you determine the correct sizes, you can order what you need in complete confidence. I'm using my seventh pair of slippers from the same mail order house. They are comfortable and fit perfectly. When one pair wears out, a check in the mail brings a new pair just like it. In time, you will have specific sources for almost all the regular items you purchase. There will be no more experimentation as with shopping because, once you find the right brand and size, you can order repeatedly.

● *Check the Back of Specialty Magazines*

One of the best ways to comparison shop for an item is to buy a specialty magazine covering that industry and examine the mail order ads in back. Photography magazines have a score of retailer ads which list specific prices for various camera equipment. You can shop for prices in several minutes. Nearly any of the ads list lower prices than you can obtain locally. Another item this works for is racquet equipment. The tennis magazines are filled with mail order ads listing prices for various quality racquets at heavy discounts.

● *Write for Information*

For a catalog specialty mail order house, write for a price on a specific item. Most of the heavier discounters are working so close to costs they won't list prices in the catalog. They prefer to move prices up and down based upon recent wholesale costs. The price quote you receive is usually good for a stated period of time. If you delay your purchase, you will have to obtain another quote.

● *Make It Easy for Mail Order Firms to Reply*

A good idea is to make it easy for the mail order house to reply to your order or to your inquiries.

Enclose a self-addressed postcard with your order. On the back print:

Your order has been received on _____ (date)

It will be shipped within _____ days.

Remarks _____

_____

Signed _____

Title _____

Date _____

This way the mail order house can let you know when to expect your order. Otherwise, you must sit and hope nothing is going wrong and that your order will be shipped within the expected time period.

● Retain Copies of Documents

Keep a copy of your order, and write down the check number and the date the order was sent. Paying by check is important because the canceled check is your proof of purchase. These items allow you to verify order and payment should a problem arise.

● Stamp the Back of the Check

Another protection for you is to stamp the back of the check, "Paid in full when endorsed." You can buy this rubber stamp for under $10. It may save you much more. What happens occasionally is that a company will change prices. If your order is shipped after a price change, they charge you the higher amount. If you have received your check with the above stamp on it, the company cannot charge you a higher price. You have proof of full payment. It's the same principle an insurance company uses when it prints, "Claim paid in full when endorsed."

● *Keep Unordered Items as Gifts*

Never pay for an item that was sent to you without being ordered. Anything sent without your request is legally considered a gift and can be kept. If a company requests payment, demand to see a proof of order. The item may have been ordered by someone else as a prank, in which case you can return it. But if there is no proof of order, then Christmas came early this year.

● *Know Your Rights*

The FTC established mail order rules in 1975. Companies selling by mail must follow certain guidelines:

1. You must receive the merchandise when the seller says you will.

2. If you are not promised delivery within a certain time period, the seller must ship the goods no later than thirty days after your order is received.

3. If the seller cannot ship within thirty days, you must be notified what the new shipping date will be, and given the option to cancel the order. The seller must also give you a free way to send back your answer. (If you don't answer, it means you agree to the delay.)

4. If you cancel a prepaid order, the seller must mail your refund within seven business days.

Mail order is an $80 billion business and growing yearly. It offers great savings but also pitfalls. Your safest approach is to deal with firms who have offered good service to you or others in the past. You can always check with your BBB before spending your money if you have any doubts.

■ BARGAINING FOR A DEAL

The U.S. is not one of the great bargaining nations. We are characterized in diplomatic circles as being one of the few nations in history to declare wars with no means to fight them, build the fighting equipment, win the wars, and then give away the fruits of the victory at the peace table. As individuals, we work much harder for a deal than people in other countries but to less effect. With our supermarkets and shopping centers, we go from store to store looking for the best price rather than bargain for the best price at a single store. The give and take of negotiating a price is a time-honored tradition overseas. It is not only essential; it is anticipated and enjoyed.

● *Use the Whistle Technique*

Don't forget the whistle technique when you hear the asking price. "Whew!" you say. Then ponder the item in silence. If you are then asked to make an opening bid, come in about the same amount lower than you think the item's worth.

● *Use the Initialed Note Technique*

If the seller makes any promises such as a guaranteed return, or statements about the background of the item or about its functioning, get the writing. To accomplish this, note whatever promises are made on a notepad, then ask the seller to just initial the sheet. Astute business people will recognize that they are signing a contract. If the seller refuses, take your business elsewhere. If you obtain the initials, then you have a written guarantee of the terms. This is an excellent all-purpose negotiating tool.

Item & Month(s)	*Item & Month(s)*
Air conditioners—2, 8	Home, vacation—8, 9
Appliances, major—1, 2, 6, 7, 11	north; 2, 3 south
Appliances, small—1	Infant needs—12
Auto, new—1, 2, 9	Jewelry—1
Auto, used—11, 12	Lamps—8
Bicycle—1, 10	Linens—1, 2, 5, 8
Books—1	Luggage—3
Building material—6, 7	Mattresses—2, 8
Carpeting—4, 5	Outdoor equipment—9
Coats—4, 9	Paint—8, 9
Department stores—2, 8	School clothes—10, 11
Fabrics—11	Shoes—2, 7, 11, 12
Fans—8	Stereo—6, 7
Furniture—1, 2, 7, 8	Storm windows—3
Furs—1, 2	Television—6, 7
Garden tractors—3, 8	Tires—4, 5
Glassware—10	Towels—1, 5, 8
Hardware—8	Washer/Drier—3
Home, residence—1, 2	Winter equipment—2, 9

WHEN TO BUY
TABLE 8-1

■ WHEN TO BUY RETAIL ITEMS

It is frustrating to bring home an item only to find it on sale the following week. Most retail merchants offer sales to reduce inventory before the new stock comes in and after the peak demand period is over. In general, postseason sales offer the greater savings items. The numbers in the following table represent the months of the year sales are most likely to be held. You might check with your retailer to see what their sales plans are. Most are happy to let you know what programs are planned and which items will be on sale.

■ CONSUMER BOOKS

The federal government has a free booklet which lists federal, state, local, and private organizations that can offer help with consumer problems. The booklet packs a wealth of valuable information into seventy-six pages. For a copy write: Consumer Resources Handbook, Dept. 635-H, Pueblo, CO 81009.

You can obtain a copy of the rules pertaining to door-to-door sales by writing: The Trade Regulation Rule Concerning a Cooling-Off Period for Door-to-Door Sales, Legal and Public Records, FTC, 6th & Pennsylvania Avenues, Washington, D.C. 20580.

■ MISCELLANEOUS HINTS

Following are more consumer hints (once again in no particular order of importance):

● *Utilize Specialty Schools*

Low cost services are often available at various educational institutions in your area. A major culinary institute in one city offers banquets to the public at reasonable prices and is booked over a year in advance. You can obtain low cost dentistry, auto repair, appliance repair, or technical services from colleges and technical schools. Check your Yellow Pages for a list of schools and then call to see what services are available. The schools often have difficulty finding customers and welcome your business. The quality of work is frequently higher than you might obtain elsewhere, as it is supervised by trained instructors and done with textbook precision.

● *Build a Rain Check File*

Getting a rain check for an out-of-stock sale item is a common pet peeve to most people. One woman actually shops late to accumulate rain checks. Whenever she spots an item that she thinks *might* be useful, that might make a good gift, or that a neighbor or friend is looking for, she makes a note of it. She then visits the store toward the end of the sale period in hopes the item will be out of stock. If so, she obtains a rain check and adds it to her file.

Sometimes she is called by the store, sometimes not. Whenever she decides to buy something, she first reviews her rain check file to see if she has any price guarantee "in stock" before shopping. If so, she calls to make certain the store now has the item and then purchases it at the lower price. While some checks go out of date, she nearly always buys at a sale price.

● *Get Credits for Christmas Returns*

Another way to save money is to request credits for returned Christmas gifts instead of buying something else right after the holidays. Although many stores have some sales the shopping days after the holidays, they don't have their big sales until mid-January. By delaying several weeks you will be trading in goods at full price in order to purchase goods at sale price two weeks later.

● *Don't Play Your Coupon Early*

Whenever you are using a discount coupon, keep it quiet until the last moment. For example, if you have a coupon for $10 off toward any automobile repair work, don't present the coupon until paying the bill. If you mention the coupon when getting an estimate, you run the risk of having the mechanic automatically adjust the estimate upward. Read the details carefully to see if there are any restrictions. Some dinner coupons require you to notify the waiter of the coupon when you order.

● *When to Grocery Shop*

Fighting crowds at the grocery store is another common pet peeve. Nothing is more aggravating than getting up to the front only to find two checkers on duty and the Democratic National Convention waiting in line. If you don't have an all-night grocery and can't shop in the middle of the night, the best time to go is during the evening meal time. The late commuters are still in their autos, families have sat down to eat, workers are relaxed reading the paper, and you are in the store. (Eat before you go. Hunger will make you buy more.)

Store managers bring the evening clerks on about 6:00 P.M., even though the rush doesn't start until later. If you begin shopping about 5:30 P.M., you will be completing just as the clerks come on duty. Yet the other customers will be starting to arrive. This is your best opportunity to avoid the crowds. The only exception is Thursday and Friday evenings. These are paydays, and the store is crowded with check cashers.

● *Be Assertive in Line*

If you are in the express line and the person in front of you has twenty items, don't be afraid to speak up. Say something to the person. Most checkers will handle them without a word. Tell the manager, who is usually near the express lane. Let the manager know that you don't appreciate being forced to wait because the rules aren't enforced.

Another injustice is waiting fifteen minutes in line only to have a clerk in the adjacent lane open up. The minute she says, "I'm open to check someone out," the land stampede starts. Invariably, the first person in the new line is someone who just walked up or who was the last person in your line. The fair procedure is for the clerk to ask the next person to be served to change lines. The people behind can then move over as they see fit. If this doesn't happen, as the checker is removing the chain, push over and state, "I've been waiting the longest. Excuse me, I'm next." Invariably the embarrassment rule takes hold and you will be waited on. I've won some dirty looks, but I get my turn.

"As I understand it, sport is hard work for which you do not get paid."

–Irvin S. Cobb

9

Filling Up on R & R

The leisure industry is in the midst of a tremendous growth boom. All those former war babies in their thirties are entertaining each other and pounding their bodies into shape in record numbers. With this boom has come the typical peak patterns we've seen in nearly every other facet of life so far. With limited facilities facing strong demand, gaining access to R & R is a job for the insider.

■ THE OFF-PEAK SPORTING LIFE

Most popular sports have regular patterns of usage. Many clubs recognize this and set prices higher for peak demand and lower when facilities are not full. This "prime" and "nonprime" pricing philosophy clearly establishes how the crowd behaves.

Racquetball

Racquetball is a winter sport. No one wants to be bouncing an innocent little ball around four walls when there are unused rays outside waiting to fall on a body. The winter season sees heavy demand. Getting a court at the last minute is possible only when you can find off-peak time.

Weekdays are nearly always open for play. Some clubs schedule women's leagues in the mornings, which can fill up the courts. Afternoons are nearly always open because the homemakers have to get back for the kiddies' naps and the working people are still chained to a desk. Weeknights (including Friday) from 5:00 P.M. until closing are normally solid with permanent time booked by the season. Daytime on the weekends is also completely booked.

Saturday and Sunday nights are usually light if there isn't a party scheduled, which block-books the courts. Racquetball is a Friday night "let's sweat and throw down some beer afterward" sport. Saturday is a "let's go out for a nice evening" night. Racquetball perspiration isn't on the program. Sunday evening is more for the family and getting ready for work the next day. So these are good times to get a court.

Tennis

To listen to the tennis players, racquetball is to tennis what roller skating is to ice skating. You won't ever see Peggy Fleming bopping down Ventura Boulevard on roller skates with a radio stuck to the side of her head. Nor will the tennis player deign to jam his body into a box and run it to death. Seriously snobbish tennis players consider the game a "country club" activity while they view racquetball as more of an "athletic club" sport.

What this means is that the Saturday night slowdown at the racquetball club is the crowded party night at a tennis club. Tennis is a couple's sport suitable for a Saturday night outing. The remaining week's schedule is very similar to the racquetball club. For either racquet sport, you have a fair chance of finding a cancellation around dinner-time. People seem to occasionally prefer filling their bellies to emptying their pores.

Bowling

Any time in the summer is good for getting a lane. The alleys are virtually deserted. During the season an open bowling lane is difficult to find because of the leagues. There are even weekday leagues because of night shift workers and homemakers. The only times you can hope to find empty lanes at most bowling alleys are Monday and Friday during the day or Monday through Thursday in the morning. All other times will be locked up with leagues.

Golf

The slowest day of the week is Tuesday. A good weekday tee time is 3:00 P.M. Most golfers will take a half day off to work in a round. The morning golfer gives way to the noontime players. At 3:00 P.M. it is a bit too early for those skipping out from work to get on the course. So you are right in between groups of players. Weekends are alway busy from dawn to dusk.

Boating

Boating enthusiasts know that Sunday is a boaters' holiday. Sunday afternoon at the average lake makes the D-day landing at Normandy look like Lewis and Clark in a canoe. We've actually pulled our boat out of the water because the lake was too crowded to even get the boat up to planing speed.

For some unknown reason, the same lakes that are swarming on Sundays are deserted on Saturdays.

Sunday is family day while Saturday is a workday. We now go on Saturdays and normally share the same lake described above with only six or seven boats. If you can take a vacation day to go during the week, you will have to share the water only with the fish.

■ THEME PARKS

The original Disneyland proved that a theme park was a veritable gold mine if properly executed. Now theme parks are a common sight in all parts of the country, with the majority in the warmer states where they can stay open year around.

● *Time Your Arrival to Miss the Crowd*

The worst days of the week depend upon the location of the theme park. It came as a surprise, but the slowest days at Disney World in Orlando are on the *weekend*. The reason is that the majority of visitors to Disney World come by car. No population centers are very near Orlando, so families must spend a day or two driving there. Leaving Saturday morning, a family with children can expect to arrive sometime Sunday or Monday. The same families face the return trip and must be back by Monday for work. So they depart before the weekend.

Theme parks near population centers see just the opposite pattern. They are within minutes of their customers who come out for the day. These parks also schedule special events to pull repeat visits out of the same population. For these parks, Friday night and all day Saturday and Sunday are extremely busy.

● *Go During an Event*

If the theme park has adequate traffic handling capabilities for extremely large crowds, it sometimes pays to go during an event such as a Senior Night when a well-known group is appearing. Waiting lines for rides are shorter then than during any other weekend time. The traffic will scare away the regular visitors and the concert-goers will be packed into the stadium. As long as you can get into or out of the place with your car, you will enjoy the park in an uncrowded condition.

● *Pick the Slowest Days*

The slowest two days of the week at a metropolitan theme park are Wednesday and Thursday. This is when to spend the day. Plan to take off from work and miss the crowds.

● *Always Bear Left*

Another idea attributed to the Disney folks is the winding serpentine line technique. The early crowds at theme parks complained of the long lines getting into the rides. The human factors engineers came up with the idea of winding lines back and forth so that more people would be within sight of the rides and the wait would appear shorter. At Disney World, the rides are designed for two lines, each winding separately.

When faced with the choice of taking the left side or the right side, always bear left. The U.S. is a right-hand driving country, and most people automatically veer right. The best illustration for this is the Space Mountain ride at Disney World. After walking up a long aisle to the top of the ride, you are forced to choose a side and your ticket is taken. But the lines themselves are around a corner out of sight. Invariably, the left-hand line is about one third shorter than the right. (The only ride this doesn't work for is the Grand Prix race course. It is designed so that the right-hand line is shorter, even when there appears to be more people waiting.)

Veering to the left works anywhere. When the crowd waiting in the lobby is allowed to enter the movie theater, more people will choose the right aisle. Stick to the left and you will have a better choice of seats.

▇ ENTERTAINMENT

Fighting the crowds at an entertainment event is another hassle. Heaven help you if your kids want to see the latest *Star Wars* movie the first two weeks or get into a Screaming Meemies rock concert. Yet there are a few tricks you can try.

● *Beat the Crowd*

The ideal time to buy tickets to a sell-out movie is a half hour after the movie starts. Between shows the traffic is catastrophic. A movie theater really needs twice as much parking as it uses for each show. This is because between shows the lot has to handle the cars of the people coming out of the movie and also the people coming to the next show. In practice, theaters have at most 50 percent more than one show requires.

If you come a half hour after the show starts, the departing crowd will have disappeared and the current crowd will be inside. With most movies lasting about two hours, you will be too early for the next show's crowd. There should be parking spots empty near the ticket office window. Buy tickets for the next show and repair to the nearest pub for a bit of refreshment or sustenance. Then plan on returning to the theater in about an hour with ticket in hand. You will have avoided the long ticket line.

Some theaters are even selling tickets one day in advance for the blockbuster sellouts. If you will be in the area, get your tickets in the daytime for an evening show and once again miss the crowds.

● *Getting into an Event at the Last Minute*

If you are desperate to see an event, whether a sporting contest or theatrical production, you can always take a chance and go to the ticket office about an hour before showtime. Often someone will be unable to attend and try to return the tickets. Refunds are not available, so the person may leave a name and number should anyone request tickets. Or you may find someone trying to get rid of extra tickets at the last minute. Depending on the demand, you may have to pay a premium to a scalper. But as start time draws near, the price will magically drop. This is a supply vs. demand problem. If the show is sold out but not a raging hit the jet set is flying in for, then you stand a good chance of getting in without having to pay a premium.

● *Beat the Crown Getting In*

After the deaths at the Who rock concert in Cincinnati, there is an excellent argument for not trying to beat the crowd into an event. The problem there was the seating scheme. Beware any time you buy tickets for an event with "festival seating." This means the organizers are trying to pack as many bodies as possible into a limited space. Instead of being given seats, the audience has to rush into an open area to fend for itself. Think carefully before you or your children go to an event with this type of seating.

If you are trying to work through a large crowd in front of a narrow entrance, such as doors to a theater or turnstiles at a football stadium, try working your way along the wall. Most people don't like the hemmed-in feeling of having the crowd on one side and the wall on the other. The people density is thinner there and you will move toward the opening faster. In general, you will get through in about one fourth the time it would take starting at the back of the crowd.

● *Getting People in Front to Sit Down*

A common pet peeve is people who stand up at events and block the view from behind. All it takes is one yo-yo up front and 100 rows of people in back are standing up to see. Then the adjacent sections stand up to see what they are missing and within no time at all an entire side is upright. The fans on the other side see all the other people standing and think they, too, are overlooking some tad of excitement and jump to their feet in anticipation. While all this is going on the only action on the field is the coach spitting wads of saliva and tobacco while the quarterback listens to the earphones during a time-out.

If you are at any public gathering where the people are supposed to be sitting but keep standing up in your way, try this offbeat trick. Wait until there are a few seconds of quiet and yell, "Quick, every-body stand up!" People will turn with a blank or puzzled look while they're sitting down and then realize you're putting them on. Believe it or not they actually think twice about standing up again! This is particularly good at sporting events. The seed you've planted keeps people firmly placed on their learning centers.

■ GAMBLING

The legal and illegal gaming business is booming. Industry experts suggest that gambling is now where the fast-food industry was twenty years ago. With casino gambling now legal in Nevada and New Jersey, and under consideration in dozens of other states, and with pari-mutuel wagering legal in many others, gambling is here to stay. What the average bettor does not know is that there are vast differences in the quality of gambling opportunities. Some wagering situations are foolhardy, while some can actually be money-makers.

The table shows the expected player advantage in various gambling situations. The percentages are supplied courtesy of John Luckman at the Gamblers Book Club in Las Vegas. Where no exact figure applies, John provided an estimate of the average, which is the figure shown in parentheses. Any nega-tive percentage represents a losing bet for the player.

Blackjack

This is the only casino game in which the player actually has an advantage over the house. The tech-

Game	Gambling Odds
Blackjack	+2% to −5.5% (0.0%)
Baccarat	−1.1% to −1.2%
Craps	−1.4% to −16.7%
Roulette	−1.4% (imprison feature)
	−2.7% (single zero)
	−5.3% (double zero)
Football & Basketball	−4.5%
Chuck-a-Luck	−8%
Slot Machines	−2.7% to −15% (−9%)
Poker	−10%
Baseball	−2% to −20% (−10%)
Wheel of Fortune	−8% to −26% (−13%)
Pari-mutuel Wagering	−14% to −19% (−17%)
Keno	−25%
Bingo	−20% to −50% (−25%)
State Lotteries	−50%
18¢ Lotteries	−90%

Percentages courtesy John Luckman,
Gamblers Book Club.

Table 9-1

nique involves a simple procedure for tracking the cards (called counting) and determining how to play hands and when to make the bets. Every insider's tip I know as a professional blackjack player is included in a book I coauthored with Lance Humble, *The World's Greatest Blackjack Book* (Doubleday, 1980). Anyone who wants to gamble for very long had better learn blackjack or have a regular source of spare funds.

Baccarat

This card game offers a fairly small disadvantage to the player. In the casino, the baccarat pit is the one with several house men in evening clothes and with very few players. Baccarat has never caught on in the U.S. because there is little for the player to do. No playing decisions other than betting the player or bank hands are required. Should you wish to play, backing the bank hand offers the lower of the two odds against you.

Craps

This is the second most popular game in the U.S. It has the interaction that Americans love. Action at the craps table is fast and furious with lots of noise. A craps game is like a pack of dogs at a flea convention. There's always lots of picking and scratching going on. While the odds against the players vary from not too bad to awful, depending upon the bet, the most accurate summary of playing craps was given by legendary gambler, Nick the Greek: "The best bet on the craps table is the *don't pass* line, and I've only lost $6 million playing it."

Roulette

This is another game which is popular in Europe but has not really caught on in the U.S. The main reason is that U.S. casinos are about twice as greedy as their European counterparts. The primary difference in advantage comes from whether or not a wheel contains one or two zeros. The European wheel has only one zero while the U.S. version has two. In addition, some overseas casinos offer an "imprison" feature, in which you don't lose your bet on the first zero spin. Your bet is imprisoned until the next spin. This reduces the casino advantage further.

Football and Basketball

More money is bet on the Super Bowl, both legally and illegally, than any other event in the U.S. Billions of dollars change hands every football season. Money is also bet on basketball, but not in the volumes of football. The bookie's advantage is developed from the fact that you must bet $11 to win $10. This is called the bookie's "vigorish."

Chuck-a-Luck

This game *looks* like a good bet for the player. In reality, there is a substantial advantage for the house. The game is played with three dice in a cage. While there are different kinds of bets allowed, the main idea is to predict what number will appear on one or more of the dice. A better name for this game is Chump-a-luck.

Slot Machines

Diamonds may be a girl's best friend, but a slot machine is a regular companion. The payoff percentage is determined by the house and constantly monitored by maintenance personnel. Some slots return as much as 97.3 percent to the players, others as low as only 85 percent. Generally, the most liberal slots are found in downtown Reno, downtown Las Vegas, and on the south shore at Tahoe.

The easiest way to locate a potentially liberal slot is to ask the one person in the casino who should know, the change girl who makes payoffs. Give her a tip and ask that she point out a slot for you. Promise that, should you win, you will be back to reward her. Make a point of taking her name down. If you do win, keep your promise. Word will get around and you will have plenty of helpful advice.

A common location for more liberal slots is near the door or near where people pass by. The theory is that casinos want passersby to see and hear money being won so that they will stop and try their hand (and wallets) too. One thing to avoid in picking a slot machine is playing the slot next to where you are winning. Casino executives often place a lower paying slot next to a liberal one. They figure that people often simultaneously play slots next to each other, or will switch machines, starting on the one nearby. In doing so, people take the winnings of one and dump them into the other.

Poker

A recent feature has been the casino poker room. Publicity generated by various poker tournaments helped create a demand for places to play. The casino runs the game and takes 10 percent of each pot, up to a maximum which varies from house to house. Find out the maximum before you sit down. As a word of warning, casino poker is very competitive. Las Vegas is loaded with full-time gamblers who love to take out-of-town hotshots and strip them clean. Also beware of private games. Poker experts have been known to band together to form a special game for a wealthy visitor. Whoever wins the mark's money splits it with the rest later on.

Baseball

The exact odds on baseball vary depending upon many handicapping factors. Generally, you are betting only when a specified pitcher works against a specific team. If that pitcher doesn't start, the bets are off.

Wheel of Fortune

This is a misnomer for the player, truth in advertising for the house. Every casino seems to have one of these arcane gizmos to add a little bit of "Gunsmoke" to the atmosphere. Tourists are about the only ones who play these things. Any knowledgeable gambler would rather bet on another Evel Knievel canyon jump first.

Pari-mutuel Wagering

You pay a hefty price in operating expenses, profit, and taxes with almost any pari-mutuel wager. The horse, dog, Jai Alai, or harness bettor can never hope to do more than watch his money as it goes by.

Keno

The only good thing about Keno is that you don't have to move. An attractive young lady will pick up your money and bets and occasionally return something. While the payoffs are sometimes enormous, the average house take is a hefty 25 percent. If you have nothing better than Keno to do with your money, buy a square inch of Elvis Presley's estate.

Bingo

Bingo is another gaming rip-off. No specific percentage is available because the exact sponsor cut depends upon the number of players.

State Lotteries

An analyst once determined that you have a better chance of being hit twice by lightning than winning certain lotteries. State lotteries have not been as successful as hoped because of the horrendously low payback to the player. The government keeps about half of all money bet for expenses and profit. The player knows a rip-off when he or she sees it. Some illegal numbers games pay off better than the state lottery. If you want to bet a lottery, do yourself a favor and save your money to buy a bridge off some stranger.

18-Cent Lotteries

Although it isn't really considered gambling, the various promotional sweepstakes offers are lotteries. For an 18-cent stamp, you have a chance to win the grand prize. Figure out the odds on a typical magazine sweepstakes offer with a total prize package of $250,000 and 17 million entries. The math works out to about 1.5 cents per entry. So ignoring the ridiculously small odds of ever winning money, the magazine is returning only 10 percent of the money you give to the USPO. This isn't much of a bet.

Most gamblers are like the New England farmer who, when asked what he would do with a million dollars, replied, "Wall, I'd jist keep on farmin' 'til it was all gone." Think of gambling as a consumer purchase of entertainment for your gaming dollar.

You can't hope to make a good buy if you aren't educated. The world's best source of information is the Gamblers Book Club in Las Vegas. For a catalog write: GBC, Post Office Box 4115, Las Vegas, NV 89106.

■ THE ULTIMATE HINT:

When you have tried every tip in this book and have still not met with success, apply this final hint. (I can't claim credit for it—that goes to radio personality, Jerry Dimit.)

■ WHEN ALL ELSE FAILS:

BARK!

Yes, bark when you are at the end of your rope. When you have been totally frustrated in every approach you've tried, BARK at the person or thing. It does wonders. It opens doors, makes people take notice, gets people moving. Bark in a restaurant and see what kind of service results. Bark at a reluctant clerk and see the action. Bark at a salesperson and watch your message get across. If nothing else, barking is a great tension reducer and makes you feel great. I've used it many times with welcome success.

Appendix A

Contributors

Bill Aichorn
George Alexander
Mary Jane Alexander
Anne Alger
A. Archer
Don Bailey
Florence Barrale
John Barrale
Josephine Barrale
Bob Berry
Ray Bobillo
Ruth Boland
Johnny Bujnak
John & Jo Bujnak
Judy Bundy
Marc Cantin
Dawn Chellis
Trish Conyers
Esther Cooper
Larry & Phyllis Cooper
Mary Frances Cooper
Jim DeAngelo
Jerry Dimit
Marilyn Dougherty
Ron Dougherty
Jane Dreeben
Mary Masterson DuBois

Allen Duke
Phyllis Duke
(Maj.) James Eldridge
Gene Faber
Norm Folkemer
John & Karen Gentles
Earl Goodman
Frank Gornick
Harold Grothaus
Loni Hallock
Laurel Hampel
Larry Heidemann
Pat Hilderbrand
Carolyn Hofstetter
Mary Hogan
Richard Huttner
Jim Jones
Todd Kamp
Giles & Peaches
   Kavanaugh
Kay Kavanaugh
Dennis Keithly
Sherry Keithly
Bobbie Knoedelseder
Patricia Kosowan
Elmer Kowal
Igor Kusyszyn

Lena LaManna
Tom Larkin
Ruth Lippincott
John Luckman
Manchester Travel
Ida Massaglia
Paeoli & Doris
   Massaglia
Dennis Master
M. L. Mazzei
Bernice McCormack
Eleanor McDonald
Mike McKinney
Jerry McReynolds
Leon Miller
Joyce Mitchell
Jimmy Mohler
Ken Mohler
John Mossinghoff
Len Motta
Shannon Motta
Terry Niehaus
Malou Norris
Bruce Northcuff
Sheila Olhsur
Bob Ovca
Nancy Ovca

Debbie Peterson
Pamela Puricelli
Terry Puricelli
Joseph Radotinski
David Reilly
Denise Reilly
Theodore Robins
Grady Jim Robinson
Mary Salih
N. L. Salter
Dick & Kathy Sheldon
Dan Simpson
Kathy & Don Souders
Beverly Sprague
JoAnne Stephens
Joe Stephens
Rose Steidl
Fred Stuart
Bob Stuckey
Rhonda Stuckey
Tom Tramski
Dee Travaglini
Don Verbeck
Elaine Viets
Voilet Weber
Chuck Williams
Marlene Williams

Appendix B

Media Coverage

City	Station	City	Station
Albuquerque	KOB	New Orleans	WGSO
Ames	WOI	Niagara Falls	CJRN
Atlanta	WRNG	Norfolk	WNIS
Bloomington	WJBC	Omaha	KQKQ
Charlotte	WTB	Oshkosh	WYAM
Chicago	WIND	Phoenix	KTAR
Columbia	WIS	Pittsburgh	KQV
Dallas	KAA	Portland	KXL
Dallas	KLIF	Rochester	WPXN
Dallas	WFAA	Rockford	WKKN
Dallas	WFAY	Rockford	WROK
Dayton	WING	Sacramento	KGNR
Des Moines	KSO	Sacramento	KXOA
Des Moines	WHO	St. Louis	KMOX
Detroit	WXYZ	San Antonio	KTSA
Grand Rapids	WTWN	San Diego	KSDL
Hamilton	CHML	San Francisco	KSFO
Hartford	WTIC	Schenectady	WGY
Kansas City	KCMO	Seattle	KAYO
Little Rock	KARN	Seattle	KIRO
Minneapolis	KSTP	Seattle	KVI
Minneapolis	WING	Toronto	CBC
Naples	WNOG		

"How to Really Get Things Done," *St. Louis Post-Dispatch,* by Elaine Viets.

"One Man's Version of How to Beat the System," *UPI, by Alice Noble.*

Bibliography

Adams, Ronald J. and Charles Remsberg. "Streetwise Guide to Self-Protection." Pamphlet by *Family Circle* magazine, 1981.

"Bargain Hunter's Calendar." *Family Circle*, January 1981.

Birkett, Jennifer. "The Truth About Radar." *Skyworld*, February/March 1980.

Candler, Julie. "Should You Contest a Traffic Ticket?" *Woman's Day*, January 15, 1980.

Crandall, Barbara and Chuck Crandall. "25 Plants that Thrive on Neglect." *Family Circle*, April 22, 1980.

Dornsife, Rod. *The Ticket Book*. New York: Bantam, 1980.

Halen, Ellis. "Help for Home Buyers." *U.S. News & World Report*, July 14, 1980.

Harvey, Kenneth R. "Don't Sell Your Home, Swap It." *50 Plus*, July 1980.

Hilderbrand, Patricia. *Space Planning with Furniture and Equipment Cutouts*. Columbia: University of Missouri, 1980.

Klein, David. "The Generic Idea: What's In a Name?" *50 Plus*, June 1980.

LeBoeuf, Michael. "Work Less, Get More Done." *Reader's Digest*, September 1979.

"Microwave Energy Saving vs. Conventional Cooktop Study." Sales brochure. Los Angeles: Thermador, 1978.

Oddo, Sandra. "Remodeling Update." *House & Garden*, June 1980.

O'Donnel, Walter E., M.D. "When to Use the Emergency Room." *Woman's Day*, November 22, 1979.

Quint, Barbara Gilder. "Credit: The American Way of Spending." *Family Circle*, July 15, 1980.

"Shopping by Mail." FTC brochure. Washington D.C.: U.S. Government Printing Office, 1979.

Steidl, Rose E. *Functional Kitchens*. Ithaca: Cornell University Extension Bulletin, 1981.

"Ways to Stop Wasting Time on the Job." *U.S. News & World Report*, March 5, 1979.

Weaver, Peter. "Mind Your Own Money." King Features Syndicate, 1980.

Send In Your Hints

So there you have literally hundreds of hints. You know ideas which can save literally hundreds of thousands of your precious seconds. All you face now is COOPER'S LAW OF SELF-IMPROVEMENT: "Everybody wants to learn how to improve themselves as long as they really don't have to do it." The final challenge is to begin applying what you have read to your daily life. Start looking for your own corners to cut.

And, by the way, if you discover a hint you haven't seen here, help us out for any following editions of this book. Send any tips to:

> Dr. Ken Cooper
> "Always Bear Left"
> P.O. Box 1205
> Ballwin, MO 63011

Once again, the deal is the same. The person who first submits any new idea which is used in a sequel will be listed in the special contributors' section. Then you will be marginally famous like the rest of us. Good luck and hoard those seconds!

Submission of tips by readers constitutes permission for the hint to be published in any *Always Bear Left* sequel and for the reader's name to be listed in the contributors' section.

Index